WHAT'S O'CLOCK

WHAT'S O'CLOCK

BY
AMY LOWELL

JONATHAN CAPE
ELEVEN GOWER STREET LONDON

The Riverside Press

CAMBRIDGE · MASSACHUSETTS

PRINTED IN THE U.S.A.

King Richard. Ay, what's o'clock?

Buckingham.   I am thus bold.

To put your grace in mind of what you promised me.

King Richard. Well, but what is't o'clock?

Buckingham.   Upon the stroke

of ten.

King Richard. Well, let it strike.

Buckingham.   Why, let it strike?

King Richard. Because that, like a Jack, thou keep'st
                          the stroke

Betwixt thy begging and my meditation.

                    Shakespeare. King Richard III.

5525

CONTENTS

East, West, North, and South of a Man   3

Evelyn Ray   14

The Swans   24

Once Jericho   29

Merely Statement   32

Footing up a Total   34

Twenty-Four Hokku on a Modern Theme   37

The Anniversary   44

Song for a Viola d'Amore   49

Prime   52

Vespers   53

In Excelsis   54

White Currants   58

Exercise in Logic   60

Overcast Sunrise   61

Afterglow   62

A Dimension   63

Mackerel Sky   64

The On-Looker   66

Lilacs   68

Purple Grackles   75

Meeting-House Hill   82

Texas   84

Charleston. South Carolina   88

The Middleton Place   90

The Vow   92

The Congressional Library   97

Which, Being Interpreted, is as may be, or Other-
    wise   104

The Sisters   127

View of Teignmouth in Devonshire   138

Fool o' the Moon   154

Tomb Valley   158

The Green Parrakeet   167

Time's Acre   174

Sultry   179

THE ENCHANTED CASTLE   182

AUTUMN AND DEATH   184

FOLIE DE MINUIT   187

THE SLIPPERS OF THE GODDESS OF BEAUTY   191

THE WATERSHED   193

LA RONDE DU DIABLE   196

MORNING SONG, WITH DRUMS   199

A GRAVE SONG   200

A RHYME OUT OF MOTLEY   201

THE RED KNIGHT   202

NUIT BLANCHE   204

ORIENTATION   206

PANTOMIME IN ONE ACT   208

IN A POWDER CLOSET   212

ATTITUDE UNDER AN ELM TREE   214

ON READING A LINE UNDERSCORED BY KEATS IN A COPY
    OF "PALMERIN OF ENGLAND"   216

THE HUMMING-BIRDS   218

SUMMER NIGHT PIECE   220

WIND AND SILVER   221

NIGHT CLOUDS   222

FUGITIVE   223

THE SAND ALTAR   224

TIME-WEB   225

PREFACE TO AN OCCASION   226

PRIMAVERA   228

KATYDIDS   230

TO CARL SANDBURG   231

IF I WERE FRANCESCO GUARDI   234

ELEONORA DUSE   235

Thanks are due to the editors of *The North American Review*, *The Atlantic*, *The Bookman*, *The Dial*, *The Century*, *Scribner's Magazine*, *Harper's Monthly Magazine*, *The New Republic*, *The Nation*, *The Nation* London, *Poetry*, *The Anglo-French Review*, *The Double Dealer*, *The Yale Review*, *Broom*, *The Saturday Review of Literature*, *Books*, *The Literary Review*, *Voices* London, and *The International Review* for their courteous permission to reprint certain of these poems which have been copyrighted by them.

Acknowledgement should also be made to the editors of the anthologies *The Enchanted Years*, *A Miscellany of American Poetry*, and *American Poetry, 1922* for the inclusion of ten poems which were published in these collections.

WHAT'S O'CLOCK

EAST, WEST, NORTH, AND SOUTH
OF A MAN

I

HE rides a white horse,

   Mary Madonna,

Dappled as clouds are dappled,

   O Mary, Mary,

And the leather of his harness is the colour of the sky.

On his head is a casque with an azure plume

Which none may observe with unswerving eyes.

   A proud gentleman, Mary Madonna.

A knight to fill the forest, riding it cross-wise,

   O Mary, Mary.

His hoof-prints dint the beech-mast,

His plume brushes the golden leaves.

No flute man this, to sigh at a lady's elbow.

This is a trumpet fellow, proper for jousting or battle,
    Mary Madonna,

To hack an enemy to pieces, and scale his castle wall.
    O Mary, Mary,

A point for piercing, an edge for shearing, a weight for
            pounding, a voice for thundering,

And a fan-gleam light to shine down little alleys

Where twisted houses make a jest of day.

There are dead men in his hand,
    Mary Madonna,

And sighing women out beyond his thinking.
    O Mary, Mary,

He will not linger here or anywhere.

He will go about his business with an ineradicable
        complaisance,

Leaving his dead to rot, his women to weep and regret,

his sons to wax into his likeness,

Never dreaming that the absurd lie he believes in

Is a gesture of Fate forcing him to the assumption of
a vast importance

Quite other than the blazoning of ceremonial banners
to wave above a tomb.

II

Hot with oranges and purples,

In a flowing robe of a marigold colour,

He sweeps over September spaces.

Scheherezade, do you hear him,

And the clang of his scimitar knocking on the gates?

The tawny glitter of his turban,

Is it not dazzling —

With the saffron jewel set like a sun-flower in the
midst?

The brown of his face!

Aye, the brown like the heart of a sun-flower.

Who are you to aspire beyond the petals,

To touch the golden burning beneath the marigold robe?

His sash is magnificence clasped by an emerald;

His scimitar is the young moon hanging before a sunset;

His voice is the sun in mid-heaven

Pouring on whirled ochre dahlias;

His fingers, the flight of Autumn wasps through a
honey-coloured afternoon.

So, Scheherezade, he has passed the dragon fountains

And is walking up the marble stairway, stopping to
caress the peacocks.

He will lean above you, Scheherezade, like September
above an orchard of apples.

He will fill you with the sweetness of spice-fed flames.

Will you burn, Scheherezade, as flowers burn in September sunlight?

Hush, then, for flame is silence,

And silent is the penetrating of the sun.

The dragon fountains splash in the court-yards,
And the peacocks spread their tails.
There are eyes in the tails of the peacocks,
But the palace windows are shuttered and barred.

III

Pipkins, pans, and pannikins,
China teapots, tin and pewter,
Baskets woven of green rushes.
Maudlin, Jennifer, and Prue,
What is lacking in your kitchens?
Are you needing skewers or thimbles,
Spools of cotton, knots of ribbon,
Or a picture for your pantry,
Or a rag-rug for the bed-side?
Plodding, plodding, through the dusty
Lanes between the hawthorn hedges,
My green wheels all white and dusty,

I as dusty as a miller,

White as any clown among them

Dancing on the London stages.

Here I have Grimaldi's latest,

Songs and ballads, sheets of posies

For your feet to ring-a-rosy.

Songs to make you sigh and shudder,

Songs to win you bright eye-glances,

Choruses, and glees, and catches.

Do your cupboards need refilling?

Take a peep into these hampers.

I have goods to loose your purse-strings:

Smocks, and shifts, and fine clocked stockings

Aprons of a dozen sizes,

Muslin dresses sprigged and patterned.

Can you look and not be buying?

Maudlin, Jennifer, and Prue,

Here are dainties for sweetheartings,

Tinsel crackers plumped with mottoes,

Twisted barley sticks and pear-drops.

Here are ear-rings, chains, and brooches,

Choose what gift you'll have him give you.

If the sweetheart days are over,

I have silver forks and bodkins,

Leather breeches, flannel bed-gowns,

Spectacles for eyes grown feeble,

Books to read with them and candles

To light up the page of evenings.

Toys, too, to delight the children,

Rocking-horses, tops, and marbles,

Dolls with jointed arms, and flying

Kites, and hoops, and even the Royal

Game of Goose the world is playing.

When I camp out on a common,

Underneath an oak or linden,

And my horse crops at his supper,

Finding it along the hedge-rows,

Then I play at Goose with one hand

Taking sides against the other.

First my right hand holds the dice-cup,

Then my left, each has its counter.

'Tis a pastime never tires.

Coppers, coppers, for the pedlar.

Maudlin, Jennifer, and Prue,

Fare you well, I must be jogging.

Horse-bells tinkle at the lane-sides,

Green wheels growing whiter, whiter,

Lurching van of whims and whimsies

Vanishing into the distance.

IV

Who would read on a ladder?

But who can read without a ladder?

Cheerful paradox to be resolved never.

Book by book, he steps up and off to all the four
        quarters

Of all the possible distances.

Minerva have a care of him,

For surely he has none for himself.

His eyes are dim with the plague of print,

But he believes them eagle-seeing.

His spectacles have grown to his nose,

But he is unaware of the fact since he never takes them

off.

A little black cap on his head;

A rusty dressing-gown, with the quilts run together,

To keep out the cold;

A window out of which he never looks;

A chair from which he never rises.

But do you not know a wharf-side when you see it,

And are you not moved at watching the putting off of

the caravels of dream?

Food gets into his mouth by accident

As though fish swam the seas to come there,

And cattle crowded the thoroughfares to reach his lips.

If there are intermediaries, he is unconscious of them,

As he is of everything but his cat,

Who shares his vigils

And has discovered the art of projecting herself into
his visions.

He loves a thousand ladies, and foregathers with a
thousand caravans.

To-day is as remote as yesterday,

And he is avid of either with the intensity of a par-
taker of each;

He could hobnob as blithely with Julius Cæsar as with
King George or Samuel Gompers,

And his opinions on affairs of the moment are those of
an eye-witness

Although he never sets foot out-of-doors.

Indeed, Minerva, you should watch the step of this
gentleman,

For he runs so swiftly past events and monuments
it seems incredible he should not trip.

The walls of forbidden cities fall before him;

He has but to tap a sheepskin to experience kingdoms,

And circumstance drips from his fingers like dust.

An habituated eye sees much through a pin-prick,

And are not his observations folio wide?

He eats the centuries

And lives a new life every twenty-four hours,

So lengthening his own to an incalculable figure.

If you think you see only an old man mouldering between four walls,

You are greatly mistaken.

Minerva over the door could tell you better

If her stone face would speak.

Talk to him and he will not hear you;

Write a book and he knows you better than you know
yourself.

Draw the curtains, then, and bring in tea, with plenty
of buttered scones.

Since neither the old gentleman nor Minerva will
speak to us,

I think we had best ignore them and go on as we are.

EVELYN RAY

No decent man will cross a field
Laid down to hay, until its yield

Is cut and cocked, yet there was the track
Going in from the lane and none coming back.

But that was afterwards; before,
The field was smooth as a sea off shore

On a shimmering afternoon, waist-high
With bent, and red top, and timothy,

Lush with oat grass and tall fescue,
And the purple green of Kentucky blue;

A noble meadow, so broad each way
It took three good scythes to mow in a day.

Just where the field broke into a wood
A knotted old catalpa stood,

And in the old catalpa-tree
A cat-bird sang immoderately.

The sky above him was round and big
And its centre seemed just over his twig.

The earth below him was fresh and fair,
With the sun's long fingers everywhere.

The cat-bird perched where a great leaf hung,
And the great leaf tilted, and flickered, and swung.

The cat-bird sang with a piercing glee
Up in the sun-specked catalpa-tree.

He sang so loud and he sang so long
That his ears were drowned in his own sweet song.

But the little peering leaves of grass
Shook and sundered to let them pass,

To let them pass, the men who heard
Nothing the grass said, nothing the bird.

Each man was still as a shining stone,
Each man's head was a buzzing bone

Wherein two words screeched in and out
Like a grinding saw with its turn about:

"Evelyn Ray," each stone man said,
And the words cut back and forth through his head,
And each of them wondered if he were dead.

The cat-bird sang with his head cocked up
Gazing into the sky's blue cup.

The grasses waved back into place,
The sun's long fingers stroked each face,

Each grim, cold face that saw no sun.
And the feet led the faces on and on.

They stopped beside the catalpa-tree,
Said one stone face to the other: "See!"

The other face had nothing to say,
Its lips were frozen on "Evelyn Ray."

They laid their hats in the tall green grass
Where the crickets and grasshoppers pass and pass.

They hung their coats in the crotch of a pine
And paced five feet in an even line.

They measured five paces either way,
And the saws in their heads screeched "Evelyn Ray."

The cat-bird sang so loud and clear
He heard nothing at all, there was nothing to hear.

Even the swish of long legs pushing
Through grass had ceased, there was only the hushing

Of a windless wind in the daisy tops,
And the jar stalks make when a grasshopper hops.

Every now and then a bee boomed over
The black-eyed Susans in search of clover,

And crickets shrilled as crickets do:
One — two. One — two.

The cat-bird sang with his head in the air,
And the sun's bright fingers poked here and there,

Past leaf, and branch, and needle, and cone.
But the stone men stood like men of stone.

Each man lifted a dull stone hand
And his fingers felt like weaving sand,

And his feet seemed standing on a ball
Which tossed and turned in a waterfall.

Each man heard a shot somewhere
Dropping out of the distant air.

But the screaming saws no longer said
"Evelyn Ray," for the men were dead.

    *   *   *   *   *

I often think of Evelyn Ray.
What did she do, what did she say?
Did she ever chance to pass that way?

I remember it as a lovely spot
Where a cat-bird sang. When he heard the shot,
Did he fly away? I have quite forgot.

When I went there last, he was singing again
Through a little fleeting, misty rain,
And pine-cones lay where they had lain.

This is the tale as I heard it when
I was young from a man who was threescore and ten.
A lady of clay and two stone men.

A pretty problem is here, no doubt,
If you have a fancy to work it out:
What happens to stone when clay is about?

Muse upon it as long as you will,
I think myself it will baffle your skill,
And your answer will be what mine is — nil.

But every sunny Summer's day
I am teased with the thought of Evelyn Ray,
Poor little image of painted clay.
And Heigh-o! I say.
What if there be a judgment-day?

What if all religions be true,

And Gabriel's trumpet blow for you

And blow for them — what will you do?

Evelyn Ray, will you rise alone?

Or will your lovers of dull grey stone

Pace beside you through the wan

Twilight of that bitter day

To be judged as stone and judged as clay,

And no one to say the judgment nay?

Better be nothing, Evelyn Ray,

A handful of buttercups that sway

In the wind for a children's holiday.

For earth to earth is the best we know,

Where the good blind worms push to and fro

Turning us into the seeds which grow,

And lovers and ladies are dead indeed,
Lost in the sap of a flower seed.
Is this, think you, a sorry creed?

Well, be it so, for the world is wide
And opinions jostle on every side.
What has always hidden will always hide.

And every year when the fields are high
With oat grass, and red top, and timothy,
I know that a creed is the shell of a lie.

Peace be with you, Evelyn Ray,
And to your lovers, if so it may,
For earth made stone and earth made clay.

THE SWANS

THE swans float and float
Along the moat
Around the Bishop's garden,
And the white clouds push
Across a blue sky
With edges that seem to draw in and harden.

Two slim men of white bronze
Beat each with a hammer on the end of a rod
The hours of God.
Striking a bell,
They do it well.
And the echoes jump, and tinkle, and swell
In the Cathedral's carved stone polygons.

The swans float

About the moat,

And another swan sits still in the air

Above the old inn.

He gazes into the street

And swims the cold and the heat,

He has always been there,

At least so say the cobbles in the square.

They listen to the beat

Of the hammered bell,

And think of the feet

Which beat upon their tops;

But what they think they do not tell.

And the swans who float

Up and down the moat

Gobble the bread the Bishop feeds them.

The slim bronze men beat the hour again,

But only the gargoyles up in the hard blue air heed
  them.

When the Bishop says a prayer,
And the choir sing "Amen,"
The hammers break in on them there:
Clang! Clang! Beware! Beware!
The carved swan looks down at the passing men,
And the cobbles wink: "An hour has gone again."
But the people kneeling before the Bishop's chair
Forget the passing over the cobbles in the square.

An hour of day and an hour of night,
And the clouds float away in a red-splashed light.
The sun, quotha? or white, white
Smoke with fire all alight.

An old roof crashing on a Bishop's tomb,
Swarms of men with a thirst for room,

And the footsteps blur to a shower, shower, shower,

Of men passing — passing — every hour,

With arms of power, and legs of power,

And power in their strong, hard minds.

No need then

For the slim bronze men

Who beat God's hours: Prime, Tierce, None.

Who wants to hear? No one.

We will melt them, and mold them,

And make them a stem

For a banner gorged with blood,

For a blue-mouthed torch.

So the men rush like clouds,

They strike their iron edges on the Bishop's chair

And fling down the lanterns by the tower stair.

They rip the Bishop out of his tomb

And break the mitre off of his head.

"See," say they, "the man is dead;

He cannot shiver or sing.

We'll toss for his ring."

The cobbles see this all along the street

Coming — coming — on countless feet.

And the clockmen mark the hours as they go.

But slow — slow —

The swans float

In the Bishop's moat.

And the inn swan

Sits on and on,

Staring before him with cold glass eyes.

Only the Bishop walks serene,

Pleased with his church, pleased with his house,

Pleased with the sound of the hammered bell,

Beating his doom.

Saying "Boom! Boom! Room! Room!"

He is old, and kind, and deaf, and blind,

And very, very pleased with his charming moat

And the swans which float.

ONCE JERICHO

WALKING in the woods one day,

I came across a great river of rye

Sweeping up between tall pine-trees.

The grey-green heads of the rye

Jostled and flaunted

And filled all the passage with a tossing

Of bright-bearded ears,

It was very fine,

Marching and bending

Under the smooth, wide undulation of the upper
  branches of pines.

"Yi! Yi!" cried the little yellow cinquefoil.

"What is this bearded army which marches upon
  us?"

And the loosestrife called out that somebody was
      treading on its toes.

But the rye never heeded.

"Bread! Bread!" it shouted, and wagged its golden
      beards.

"Bread conquering the forest."

I stood with the little cinquefoil

Crushed back against a bush of sheep's laurel.

"I am sorry if I crowd you," said I.

"But the rye is marching

And the green and yellow banners blind me,

Also the clamour of the great trumpets

Is confusing."

"But you are trampling me down," wailed the loose-
      strife.

"Alas! Even so.

Yet do not blame me,

For I too have scarcely room to stand."

Then a gust of wind ran upon the tall rye,

And it flung up its glittering helmets and shouted
"Bread!" again and again,

And the hubbub of it rolled superbly under the balancing pines.

"Three times the trumpets," thought I,

And I picked the cinquefoil.

"Why not on my writing-table," I said, caressing its
petals with my finger.

And that, I take it, is the end of the story.

MERELY STATEMENT

You sent me a sprig of mignonette,
Cool-coloured, quiet, and it was wet
With green sea-spray, and the salt and the sweet
Mingled to a fragrance weary and discreet
As a harp played softly in a great room at sunset.

You said: "My sober mignonette
Will brighten your room and you will not forget."

But I have pressed your flower and laid it away
In a letter, tied with a ribbon knot.
I have not forgot.
But there is a passion-flower in my vase
Standing above a close-cleared space
In the midst of a jumble of papers and books.

The passion-flower holds my eyes,

And the light-under-light of its blue and purple dyes

Is a hot surprise.

How then can I keep my looks

From the passion-flower leaning sharply over the

    books?

When one has seen

The difficult magnificence of a queen

On one's table,

Is one able

To observe any colour in a mignonette?

I will not think of sunset, I crave the dawn,

With its rose-red light on the wings of a swan,

And a queen pacing slowly through the Parthenon,

Her dress a stare of purple between pillars of stone.

FOOTING UP A TOTAL

I MOVED to the sound of gold, and brass, and heavily-
  clashed silver.
From the towers, the watchers see the flags of my
  coming:
Tall magenta flags
Stinging against a pattern of light blue.
Trumpets and tubas
Exult for me before the walls of cities,
And I pass the gates entangled in a dance of lifted
  tambourines.

But you — you come only as a harebell comes;
One day there is nothing, and the next your steepled
  bells are all,
The rest is background.

You are neither blue, nor violet, nor red,

But all these colours blent and faded to a charming
  weariness of tone.

I glare; you blossom.

Yes, alas! and when they have clanged me to my grave

Wrapped gaudily in pale blue and magenta;

When muted bugles and slacked drums

Have brayed a last quietus;

What then, my friend?

Why, someone coming from the funeral

Will see you standing, nodding underneath a hedge

(Picking or not is nothing).

Will that person remember bones and shouting do you
  think?

I fancy he will listen to the music

Shaken so lightly from your whispering bells

And think how very excellent a thing

A flower growing in a hedge most surely is.

And so, a fig for rotting carcasses!

Waiter, bring me a bottle of Lachrima Christi,
And mind you don't break the seal.
Your health, my highly unsuccessful confrère,
Rocking your seed-bells while I drift to ashes.
The future is the future, therefore —
Damn you!

TWENTY-FOUR HOKKU ON A MODERN THEME

I

AGAIN the larkspur,
Heavenly blue in my garden.
They, at least, unchanged.

II

How have I hurt you?
You look at me with pale eyes,
But these are my tears.

III

Morning and evening —
Yet for us once long ago
Was no division.

IV

I hear many words.
Set an hour when I may come
Or remain silent.

V

In the ghostly dawn
I write new words for your ears —
Even now you sleep.

VI

This then is morning.
Have you no comfort for me
Cold-coloured flowers?

VII

My eyes are weary
Following you everywhere.
Short, oh short, the days!

VIII

When the flower falls
The leaf is no more cherished.
Every day I fear.

IX

Even when you smile
Sorrow is behind your eyes.
Pity me, therefore.

X

Laugh — it is nothing.
To others you may seem gay,
I watch with grieved eyes.

XI

Take it, this white rose.
Stems of roses do not bleed;
Your fingers are safe.

XII

As a river-wind

Hurling clouds at a bright moon,

So am I to you.

XIII

Watching the iris,

The faint and fragile petals —

How am I worthy?

XIV

Down a red river

I drift in a broken skiff.

Are you then so brave?

XV

Night lies beside me

Chaste and cold as a sharp sword.

It and I alone.

XVI

Last night it rained.

Now, in the desolate dawn,

Crying of blue jays.

XVII

Foolish so to grieve,

Autumn has its coloured leaves —

But before they turn?

XVIII

Afterwards I think:

Poppies bloom when it thunders.

Is this not enough?

XIX

Love is a game — yes?

I think it is a drowning:

Black willows and stars.

XX

When the aster fades
The creeper flaunts in crimson.
Always another!

XXI

Turning from the page,
Blind with a night of labour,
I hear morning crows.

XXII

A cloud of lilies,
Or else you walk before me.
Who could see clearly?

XXIII

Sweet smell of wet flowers
Over an evening garden.
Your portrait, perhaps?

XXIV

Staying in my room,

I thought of the new Spring leaves.

That day was happy.

THE ANNIVERSARY

Ten years is nothing,
Yet I do not remember
What happened before.

Morning flings shadows,
But midday is shadowless.
So I have found it.

I have no flowers,
Yet I give you these roses.
Humour my pretence.

Have I satisfied?
Who can be sure of himself.
Touch me with your love.

Knowing my weakness,
Spread your hands above my head.
See only your hands.

Watching you daily,
I dare not think what I see.
It is better so.

Since I am only
What you may consider me,
Have merciful thoughts.

Shield me from myself.
At times I have wounded you.
I do not forget.

Take what I give you.
Foolishness is in my words,
But not in my heart.

Cease urging your ears,

My speech has little for them.

Hearken otherwise.

You wrong me, saying:

One death will not kill us both.

Your veins hold my sap.

Keep in remembrance:

Peonies do not blossom

Till Spring is over.

You prefer Spring? Why?

A season's length of hours —

Incalculable.

Days and days — what then?

Is not recurrence a smile

On the face of age?

Now, in the pale dawn,
How strange to consider time.
What is it to us?

Grains of rice counted —
Can any one so spend life?
Be spacious and wise.

The bowl is still full.
We will not be niggardly.
Plunge in both your hands.

I have known terror.
I swear to know it no more,
Each day a new dawn.

Youth is incautious.
Wisdom learns to tread softly,
Valuing moments.

Cherishing what is,
The wise man sees it depart
Without emotion.

Time is rhetoric,
A mad logician's plaything.
O pitiful world!

Listen to the wind;
Man has not learnt to measure
The wind of his thought.

Blowing asunder,
Yet we shall be as the air
Still undivided.

Sleep until day-spring.
With morning we start again,
Another ten years.

SONG FOR A VIOLA D'AMORE

THE lady of my choice is bright
As a clematis at the touch of night,
As a white clematis with a purple heart
When twilight cuts earth and sun apart.
Through the dusking garden I hear her voice
As a smooth, sweet, wandering, windy noise,
And I see her stand as a ghost may do
In answer to a rendez-vous
Long sought with agony and prayer.
So watching her, I see her there.

I sit beneath a quiet tree
And watch her everlastingly.
The garden may or may not be
Before my eyes, I cannot see.

But darkness drifting up and down

Divides to let her silken gown

Gleam there beside the clematis.

How marvellously white it is!

Five white blossoms and she are there

Like candles in a fluttering air

Escaping from a tower stair.

Be still you cursed, rattling leaf,
This is no time to think of grief.

The night is soft, and fire-flies

Are very casual, gay, and wise,

And they have made a tiny glee

Just where the clematis and she

Are standing. Since the sky is clear,

Do they suppose that, once a year,

The moon and five white stars appear

Walking the earth; that, so attended,

Diana came and condescended

To hold speech with Endymion

Before she came at last alone.

The lady of my choice is bright

As a clematis at the fall of night.

Her voice is honeysuckle sweet,

Her presence spreads an April heat

Before the going of her feet.

She is of perfectness complete.

The lady whom my heart perceives

As a clematis above its leaves,

As a purple-hearted clematis.

And what is lovelier than that is?

PRIME

YOUR voice is like bells over roofs at dawn

When a bird flies

And the sky changes to a fresher colour.

Speak, speak, Beloved.

Say little things

For my ears to catch

And run with them to my heart.

VESPERS

LAST night, at sunset,

The foxgloves were like tall altar candles.

Could I have lifted you to the roof of the greenhouse,

    my Dear,

I should have understood their burning.

IN EXCELSIS

You — you —

Your shadow is sunlight on a plate of silver;

Your footsteps, the seeding-place of lilies;

Your hands moving, a chime of bells across a windless
air.

The movement of your hands is the long, golden running of light from a rising sun;

It is the hopping of birds upon a garden-path.

As the perfume of jonquils, you come forth in the
morning.

Young horses are not more sudden than your
thoughts,

Your words are bees about a pear-tree,

Your fancies are the gold-and-black striped wasps
    buzzing among red apples.

I drink your lips,

I eat the whiteness of your hands and feet.

My mouth is open,

As a new jar I am empty and open.

Like white water are you who fill the cup of my
    mouth,

Like a brook of water thronged with lilies.

You are frozen as the clouds,

You are far and sweet as the high clouds.

I dare reach to you,

I dare touch the rim of your brightness.

I leap beyond the winds,

I cry and shout,

For my throat is keen as a sword

Sharpened on a hone of ivory.

My throat sings the joy of my eyes,

The rushing gladness of my love.

How has the rainbow fallen upon my heart?

How have I snared the seas to lie in my fingers

And caught the sky to be a cover for my head?

How have you come to dwell with me,

Compassing me with the four circles of your mystic
      lightness,

So that I say "Glory! Glory!" and bow before you

As to a shrine?

Do I tease myself that morning is morning and a day
      after?

Do I think the air a condescension,

The earth a politeness,

Heaven a boon deserving thanks?

So you — air — earth — heaven —

I do not thank you,

I take you,

I live.

And those things which I say in consequence

Are rubies mortised in a gate of stone.

WHITE CURRANTS

SHALL I give you white currants?

I do not know why, but I have a sudden fancy for this
  fruit.

At the moment, the idea of them cherishes my senses,

And they seem more desirable than flawless emeralds.

Since I am, in fact, empty-handed,

I might have chosen gems out of India,

But I choose white currants.

Is it because the raucous wind is hurtling round the
  house-corners?

I see it with curled lips and stripped fangs, gaunt with
  a hunting energy,

Come to snout, and nibble, and kill the little crocus
  roots.

Shall we call it white currants?

You may consider it as a symbol if you please.

You may find them tart, or sweet, or merely agreeable
in colour,

So long as you accept them,

And me.

EXERCISE IN LOGIC

I GAVE you a picture once,

A great crimson sun floating beside a gnarled bamboo.

The sun has faded;

For which reason, I think nothing of the painter,

Until I reflect that many pigments cannot bear the
dazzle of excessive light.

For, my Dear, have you not sat opposite it daily?

I ask you, is there truth in this?

OVERCAST SUNRISE

THE sky is spattered with clouds,

Pink clouds,

And behind them is the reluctant blue of dawn.

The hemlock-trees move to a weary wind,

And the clouds lose their brightness,

Gathering to a dull day.

Morning, you observe —

But the night was more shining in my thoughts.

O realistic generation,

Who do not get abroad while still the clouds are pink

And the sky concerned only with how much colour it

      will choose to wear!

AFTERGLOW

PEONIES

The strange pink colour of Chinese porcelains;

Wonderful — the glow of them.

But, my Dear, it is the pale blue larkspur

Which swings windily against my heart.

Other Summers —

And a cricket chirping in the grass.

A DIMENSION

To-NIGHT I stood among roses

Watching the slow studding of the sky with stars.

The cat fawned upon me to play with him.

Poor little cat, you have only me,

Unless we add that delightful feather on the end of a
whip.

I have flowers and the high green loveliness of an
evening sky,

And I find them not worth your feather,

Since the earth happens to be round as an orange

And I am not possessed of seven league boots.

MACKEREL SKY

I RIDE, ride,

Through the spotted sunlight of an April forest

Down a pathway bewildered with crocus cups,

The wind dallies with the plume of my helmet.

I ride, ride,

Seeking those adventures to which I am dedicate,

Determined, but without alertness,

Ungraciously ignoring the salutations of the young,
        jocund leaves.

Lady,

Far as you are from me in distance of place,

I know you yet farther off in good will of heart.

Wherefore,

Although I make a brave show in armour of green
     and carnation
Rivetted with the flowers which are called "you-love-
     me-not" of white and yellow,
And on my shield a waning moon in a field of azure,
I am gayer in my colours than in my heart.

THE ON-LOOKER

SUPPOSE I plant you

Like wide-eyed Helen

On the battlements

Of weary Troy,

Clutching the parapet with desperate hands.

She, too, gazes at a battle-field

Where bright vermilion plumes and metal whiteness

Shock and sparkle and go down with groans.

Her glances strike the rocking battle,

Again — again —

Recoiling from it

Like baffled spear-heads fallen from a brazen shield.

The ancients at her elbow counsel patience and con-
    tingencies;

Such to a woman stretched upon a bed of battle,

Who bargained for this only in the whispering arras

Enclosed about a midnight of enchantment.

LILACS

Lilacs,

False blue,

White,

Purple,

Colour of lilac,

Your great puffs of flowers

Are everywhere in this my New England.

Among your heart-shaped leaves

Orange orioles hop like music-box birds and sing

Their little weak soft songs;

In the crooks of your branches

The bright eyes of song sparrows sitting on spotted
     eggs

Peer restlessly through the light and shadow

Of all Springs.

Lilacs in dooryards

Holding quiet conversations with an early moon;

Lilacs watching a deserted house

Settling sideways into the grass of an old road;

Lilacs, wind-beaten, staggering under a lopsided
      shock of bloom

Above a cellar dug into a hill.

You are everywhere.

You were everywhere.

You tapped the window when the preacher preached
      his sermon,

And ran along the road beside the boy going to school.

You stood by pasture-bars to give the cows good
      milking,

You persuaded the housewife that her dish pan was of
      silver

And her husband an image of pure gold.

You flaunted the fragrance of your blossoms

Through the wide doors of Custom Houses —

You, and sandal-wood, and tea,

Charging the noses of quill-driving clerks

When a ship was in from China.

You called to them: "Goose-quill men, goose-quill
men,

May is a month for flitting,"

Until they writhed on their high stools

And wrote poetry on their letter-sheets behind the
propped-up ledgers.

Paradoxical New England clerks,

Writing inventories in ledgers, reading the "Song of
Solomon" at night,

So many verses before bed-time,

Because it was the Bible.

The dead fed you

Amid the slant stones of graveyards.

Pale ghosts who planted you

Came in the night-time

And let their thin hair blow through your clustered
stems.

You are of the green sea,

And of the stone hills which reach a long distance.

You are of elm-shaded streets with little shops where
       they sell kites and marbles,

You are of great parks where everyone walks and no-
       body is at home.

You cover the blind sides of greenhouses

And lean over the top to say a hurry-word through
       the glass

To your friends, the grapes, inside.

Lilacs,

False blue,

White,

Purple,

Colour of lilac,

You have forgotten your Eastern origin,

The veiled women with eyes like panthers,

The swollen, aggressive turbans of jewelled Pashas.

Now you are a very decent flower,

A reticent flower,

A curiously clear-cut, candid flower,

Standing beside clean doorways,

Friendly to a house-cat and a pair of spectacles,

Making poetry out of a bit of moonlight

And a hundred or two sharp blossoms.

Maine knows you,

Has for years and years;

New Hampshire knows you,

And Massachusetts

And Vermont.

Cape Cod starts you along the beaches to Rhode Is-
       land;

Connecticut takes you from a river to the sea.

You are brighter than apples,

Sweeter than tulips,

You are the great flood of our souls

Bursting above the leaf-shapes of our hearts,

You are the smell of all Summers,

The love of wives and children,

The recollection of the gardens of little children,

You are State Houses and Charters

And the familiar treading of the foot to and fro on a
    road it knows.

May is lilac here in New England,

May is a thrush singing "Sun up!" on a tip-top ash-
    tree,

May is white clouds behind pine-trees

Puffed out and marching upon a blue sky.

May is a green as no other,

May is much sun through small leaves,

May is soft earth,

And apple-blossoms,

And windows open to a South wind.

May is a full light wind of lilac

From Canada to Narragansett Bay.

Lilacs,

False blue,

White,

Purple,

Colour of lilac.

Heart-leaves of lilac all over New England,

Roots of lilac under all the soil of New England,

Lilac in me because I am New England,

Because my roots are in it,

Because my leaves are of it,

Because my flowers are for it,

Because it is my country

And I speak to it of itself

And sing of it with my own voice

Since certainly it is mine.

PURPLE GRACKLES

THE grackles have come.

The smoothness of the morning is puckered with their
incessant chatter.

A sociable lot, these purple grackles,

Thousands of them strung across a long run of wind,

Thousands of them beating the air-ways with quick
wing-jerks,

Spinning down the currents of the South.

Every year they come,

My garden is a place of solace and recreation evi-
dently,

For they always pass a day with me.

With high good nature they tell me what I do not
want to hear.

The grackles have come.

I am persuaded that grackles are birds;

But when they are settled in the trees,

I am inclined to declare them fruits

And the trees turned hybrid blackberry vines.

Blackness shining and bulging under leaves,

Does not that mean blackberries, I ask you?

Nonsense! The grackles have come.

Nonchalant highwaymen, pickpockets, second-story
      burglars,

Stealing away my little hope of Summer.

There is no stealthy robbing in this.

Who ever heard such a gabble of thieves' talk!

It seems they delight in unmasking my poor pre-
      tence.

Yes, now I see that the hydrangea blooms are rusty;

That the hearts of the golden glow are ripening to
      lustreless seeds;

That the garden is dahlia-coloured,

Flaming with its last over-hot hues;

That the sun is pale as a lemon too small to fill the
picking-ring.

I did not see this yesterday,

But to-day the grackles have come.

They drop out of the trees

And strut in companies over the lawn,

Tired of flying, no doubt;

A grand parade to limber legs and give wings a rest.

I should build a great fish-pond for them,

Since it is evident that a bird-bath, meant to accom-
modate two goldfinches at most,

Is slight hospitality for these hordes.

Scarcely one can get in,

They all peck and scrabble so,

Crowding, pushing, chasing one another up the bank
with spread wings.

"Are we ducks, you, owner of such inadequate com-
forts,

That you offer us lily-tanks where one must swim or
drown,

Not stand and splash like a gentleman?"

I feel the reproach keenly, seeing them perch on the
edges of the tanks, trying the depth with a
chary foot,

And hardly able to get their wings under water in the
bird-bath.

But there are resources I had not considered,

If I am bravely ruled out of count.

What is that thudding against the eaves just beyond
my window?

What is that spray of water blowing past my face?

Two — three — grackles bathing in the gutter,

The gutter providentially choked with leaves.

I pray they think I put the leaves there on purpose;

I would be supposed thoughtful and welcoming

To all guests, even thieves.

But considering that they are going South and I am
  not,

I wish they would bathe more quietly,

It is unmannerly to flaunt one's good fortune.

They rate me of no consequence,

But they might reflect that it is my gutter.

I know their opinion of me,

Because one is drying himself on the window-sill

Not two feet from my hand.

His purple neck is sleek with water,

And the fellow preens his feathers for all the world as
  if I were a fountain statue.

If it were not for the window,

I am convinced he would light on my head.

Tyrian-feathered freebooter,

Appropriating my delightful gutter with so extrava-
  gant an ease,

You are as cool a pirate as ever scuttled a ship,

And are you not scuttling my Summer with every
peck of your sharp bill?

But there is a cloud over the beech-tree,

A quenching cloud for lemon-livered suns.

The grackles are all swinging in the tree-tops,

And the wind is coming up, mind you.

That boom and reach is no Summer gale,

I know that wind,

It blows the Equinox over seeds and scatters them,

It rips petals from petals, and tears off half-turned
leaves.

There is rain on the back of that wind.

Now I would keep the grackles,

I would plead with them not to leave me.

I grant their coming, but I would not have them go.

It is a milestone, this passing of grackles.

A day of them, and it is a year gone by.

There is magic in this and terror,

But I only stare stupidly out of the window.

The grackles have come.

Come! Yes, they surely came.

But they have gone.

A moment ago the oak was full of them,

They are not there now.

Not a speck of a black wing,

Not an eye-peep of a purple head.

The grackles have gone,

And I watch an Autumn storm

Stripping the garden,

Shouting black rain challenges

To an old, limp Summer

Laid down to die in the flower-beds.

MEETING–HOUSE HILL

I MUST be mad, or very tired,

When the curve of a blue bay beyond a railroad track

Is shrill and sweet to me like the sudden springing of
    a tune,

And the sight of a white church above thin trees in a
    city square

Amazes my eyes as though it were the Parthenon.

Clear, reticent, superbly final,

With the pillars of its portico refined to a cautious
    elegance,

It dominates the weak trees,

And the shot of its spire

Is cool, and candid,

Rising into an unresisting sky.

Strange meeting-house

Pausing a moment upon a squalid hill-top.

I watch the spire sweeping the sky,

I am dizzy with the movement of the sky,

I might be watching a mast

With its royals set full

Straining before a two-reef breeze.

I might be sighting a tea-clipper,

Tacking into the blue bay,

Just back from Canton

With her hold full of green and blue porcelain,

And a Chinese coolie leaning over the rail

Gazing at the white spire

With dull, sea-spent eyes.

TEXAS

I WENT a-riding, a-riding,
Over a great long plain.
And the plain went a-sliding, a-sliding
Away from my bridle-rein.

Fields of cotton, and fields of wheat,
Thunder-blue gentians by a wire fence,
Standing cypress, red and tense,
Holding its flower rigid like a gun,
Dressed for parade by the running wheat,
By the little bouncing cotton. Terribly sweet
The cardinals sing in the live-oak trees,
And the long plain breeze,
The prairie breeze,
Blows across from swell to swell

With a ginger smell.

Just ahead, where the road curves round,

A long-eared rabbit makes a bound

Into a wheat-field, into a cotton-field,

His track glitters after him and goes still again

Over to the left of my bridle-rein.

But over to the right is a glare — glare — glare —

Of sharp glass windows.

A narrow square of brick jerks thickly up above the
cotton plants,

A raucous mercantile thing flaring the sun from thirty-
six windows,

Brazenly declaring itself to the lovely fields.

Tram-cars run like worms about the feet of this
thing,

The coffins of cotton-bales feed it,

The threshed wheat is its golden blood.

But here it has no feet,

It has only the steep ironic grin of its thirty-six windows,
Only its basilisk eyes counting the fields,
Doing sums of how many buildings to a city, all day
   and all night.

Once they went a-riding, a-riding,
Over the great long plain.
Cowboys singing to their dogey steers,
Cowboys perched on forty-dollar saddles,
Riding to the North, six months to get there,
Six months to reach Wyoming.
"Hold up, paint horse, herd the little dogies,
Over the lone prairie."
Bones of dead steers,
Bones of cowboys,
Under the wheat, maybe.

The sky-scraper sings another way,

A tune of steel, of wheels, of gold.

And the ginger breeze blows, blows all day

Tanged with flowers and mold.

And the Texas sky whirls down, whirls down,

Taking long looks at the fussy town.

An old sky and a long plain

Beyond, beyond, my bridle-rein.

CHARLESTON. SOUTH CAROLINA

FIFTEEN years is not a long time,

But long enough to build a city over and destroy it.

Long enough to clean a forty-year growth of grass
      from between cobblestones,

And run street-car lines straight across the heart of
      romance.

Commerce, are you worth this?

I should like to bring a case to trial:

Prosperity versus Beauty,

Cash registers teetering in a balance against the com-
      fort of the soul.

Then, to-night, I stood looking through a grilled gate

At an old, dark garden.

Live-oak trees dripped branchfuls of leaves over the
      wall,

Acacias waved dimly beyond the gate, and the smell
    of their blossoms
Puffed intermittently through the wrought-iron scroll-
    work.
Challenge and solution —
O loveliness of old, decaying, haunted things!
Little streets untouched, shamefully paved,
Full of mist and fragrance on this rainy evening.
"You should come at dawn," said my friend,
"And see the orioles, and thrushes, and mocking-
    birds
In the garden."
"Yes," I said absent-mindedly,
And remarked the sharp touch of ivy upon my hand
    which rested against the wall.
But I thought to myself,
There is no dawn here, only sunset,
And an evening rain scented with flowers.

THE MIDDLETON PLACE

CHARLESTON, S.C.

WHAT would Francis Jammes, lover of dear, dead
    elegancies,

Say to this place?

France, stately, formal, stepping in red-heeled shoes

Along a river shore.

France walking a minuet between live-oaks waving
    ghostly fans of Spanish moss.

La Caroline, indeed, my dear Jammes,

With Monsieur Michaux engaged to teach her de-
    portment.

Faint as a whiff of flutes and hautbois,

The great circle of the approach lies beneath the
    sweeping grasses.

Step lightly down these terraces, they are records of
    a dream.

Magnolias, pyrus japonicas, azaleas,

Flaunting their scattered blooms with the same bra-
vura

That lords and ladies used in the prison of the Con-
ciergerie.

You were meant to be so gay, so sophisticated, and
you are so sad,

Sad as the tomb crouched amid your tangled growth,

Sad as the pale plumes of the Spanish moss

Slowly strangling the live-oak trees.

Sunset wanes along the quiet river.

The afterglow is haunted and nostalgic,

Over the yellow woodland it hangs like the dying
chord of a funeral chant;

And evenly, satirically, the mosses move to its inef-
fable rhythm,

Like the ostrich fans of palsied dowagers

Telling one another contentedly of the deaths they
have lived to see.

THE VOW

TREAD softly, softly,

Scuffle no dust.

No common thoughts shall thrust

Upon this peaceful decay,

This mold and rust of yesterday.

This is an altar with its incense blown away

By the indifferent wind of a long, sad night;

These are the precincts of the dead who die

Unconquered. Haply

You who haunt this place

May deign some gesture of forgiveness

To those of our sundered race

Who come in all humility

Asking an alms of pardon.

Suffer us to feel an ease,

A benefice of love poured down on us from these magnolia-trees.

That, when we leave you, we shall know the bitter
wound

Of our long mutual scourging healed at last and sound.

Through an iron gate, fantastically scrolled and gar-
landed,

Along a path, green with moss, between two rows of
high magnolia-trees —

How lightly the wind drips through the magnolias.

How slightly the magnolias bend to the wind.

It stands, pushed back into a corner of the piazza,

A jouncing-board, with its paint scaled off,

A jouncing-board which creaks when you sit upon
it.

The wind rattles the stiff leaves of the magnolias:

So may tinkling banjos drown the weeping of women.

When the Yankees came like a tide of locusts,

When blue uniforms blocked the ends of streets

And foolish, arrogant swords struck through the
paintings of a hundred years.

*From gold and ivory coasts come the winds that jingle
in the tree-tops;*

*But the sigh of the wind in the unshaven grass, from
whence is that?*

Proud hearts who could not endure desecration,

Who almost loathed the sky because it was blue;

Vengeful spirits, locked in young, arrogant bodies,

You cursed yourselves with a vow:

Never would you set foot again in Charleston
streets,

Never leave your piazza till Carolina was rid of Yankees.

O smooth wind sliding in from the sea,

It is a matter of no moment to you what flag you are
        flapping.

Ocean tides, morning and evening, slipping past the
        sea-islands;
Tides slipping in through the harbour, shaking the
        palmetto posts,
Slipping out through the harbour;
Pendulum tides, counting themselves upon the sea-
        islands.

So they jounced, for health's sake,
To be well and able to rejoice when once again the
        city was free,
And the lost cause won, and the stars and bars afloat
        over Sumter.
The days which had roared to them called more softly,
The days whispered, the days were silent, they moved
        as imperceptibly as mist.

And the proud hearts went with the days, into the
        dusk of age, the darkness of death.

Slowly they were borne away through a Charleston
        they scarcely remembered.

The jouncing-board was pushed into a corner,

Only the magnolia-trees tossed a petal to it, now and
        again, if there happened to be a strong wind
        when the blooms were dropping.

Hush, go gently,

Do not move a pebble with your foot.

This is a moment of pause,

A moment to recollect the futility of cause.

A moment to bow the head

And greet the unconcerned dead,

Denying nothing of their indifference,

And then go hence

And forget them again,

Since lives are lived with living men.

THE CONGRESSIONAL LIBRARY

THE earth is a coloured thing.

See the red clays, and the umbers and salt greys of the
    mountains;

See the clustered and wandering greens of plains and
    hillsides,

The leaf-greens, bush-greens, water-plant and snow-
    greens

Of gardens and forests.

See the reds of flowers — hibiscus, poppy, geranium;

The rose-red of little flowers — may-flowers, prim-
    roses;

The harlequin shades of sweet-peas, orchids, pansies;

The madders, saffrons, chromes, of still waters,

The silver and star-blues, the wine-blues of seas and
    oceans.

Observe the stars at night time, name the colour of
    them;

Count and recount the hues of clouds at sunset and at
    dawn.

And the colours of the races of men —

What are they?

And what are we?

We, the people without a race,

Without a language;

Of all races, and of none;

Of all tongues, and one imposed;

Of all traditions and all pasts,

With no tradition and no past.

A patchwork and an altar-piece,

Vague as sea-mist,

Myriad as forest-trees,

Living into a present,

Building a future.

Our colour is the vari-coloured world.

No colours clash,

All clash and change,

And, in changing, new colours come and go and domi-
      nate and remain,

And no one shall say which remain,

Since those that have vanished return,

And those no man has seen take the light and are.

Where else in all America are we so symbolized

As in this hall?

White columns polished like glass,

A dome and a dome,

A balcony and a balcony,

Stairs and the balustrades to them,

Yellow marble and red slabs of it,

All mounting, spearing, flying into colour.

Colour round the dome and up to it,

Colour curving, kite-flying, to the second dome,

Light, dropping, pitching down upon the colour,

Arrow-falling upon the glass-bright pillars,

Mingled colours spinning into a shape of white pillars,

Fusing, cooling, into balanced shafts of shrill and
        interthronging light.

This is America,

This vast, confused beauty,

This staring, restless speed of loveliness,

Mighty, overwhelming, crude, of all forms,

Making grandeur out of profusion,

Afraid of no incongruities,

Sublime in its audacity,

Bizarre breaker of moulds,

Laughing with strength,

Charging down on the past,

Glorious and conquering,

Destroyer, builder,

Invincible pith and marrow of the world,

An old world remaking,

Whirling into the no-world of all-coloured light.

But behind the vari-coloured hall?

The entrails, the belly,

The blood-run veins, the heart and viscera,

What of these?

Only at night do they speak,

Only at night do the voices rouse themselves and
      speak.

There are words in the veins of this creature,

There are still notes singing in its breast:

Silent voices, whispering what it shall speak,

Frozen music beating upon its pulses.

These are the voices of the furious dead who never die,

Furious with love and life, unquenchable,

Dictating their creeds across the vapours of time.

This is the music of the Trumpeters of the Almighty

Weeping for a lost estate,

Sounding to a new birth which is to-morrow.

Hark! This hurricane of music has no end,

The speech of these voices has neither end nor begin-
        ning;
They are inter-riven as the colours of the sky
Over the graveyards of ten thousand generations.

When we are as Nineveh, our white columns thrown
        and scattered,
Our dome of colours striped with the crawling of in-
        sects,
Spotted with the thrust of damp clay —
Our words, our music, who will build a dome to hive
        them?
In whose belly shall we come to life?
A new life,
Beyond submergence and destruction,
The implacable life of silent words,
Of tumultuous stillness of never-ceasing music,
Lost to being that so it may triumph
And become the blood and heat and urge

Of that hidden distance which forever whips and har-
        ries the static present
Of mankind.

WHICH, BEING INTERPRETED, IS AS MAY BE, OR OTHERWISE

UNDERNEATH the dim, criss-crossing beams

Grown edgeless with the litter of decay,

Where spiders hung their everlasting webs

To wave, tier upon tier, across the gloom

Whenever any little cranny wind

Whined in on them and tumbled up the dust

Upon the flaking beams and on the floor

Startling the nosing rats to sudden cold,

Old Neron sat, cuddling his withered bones.

Above his head, the great Cathedral bells

Scattered their hallelujahs round the sky

On Sundays, holy days, and festivals;

But Neron took no note of them, his ears

Were inadvertent to such happenings

As cry themselves with bells. He sat unmoved,

Scuffing his naked feet in the thick dust

Poured from the mouldering beams by the bells' jar,

Sorting his pleasure from old heaps of thoughts.

Below his garret, stairs and stairs below,

Men skinned their fingers tugging at the ropes

That swung the clappers of the chiming bells.

No kith nor kin to Neron, these; his bones

Were liker to the shafts and traceries

And gargoyled gutters shining on the town

In twitched and twisted angles. Neron paid

No least attention to them, nor the church

Which harboured him; and yet it was a jewel,

A very rose of Gothic merriment,

Blooming symbolic beasts on every arch

And sprouting columns like a Summer wood.

All up and down were flights of spiral stairs,

Contrived within the hollow core of walls,

Leading to chambers of hewn stone, and lofts

Where slits for windows pierced the granite blocks

More than an arm's length to reach open air,

And distant so far down that sums of steps

Ran into figures to affright the mind,

God lived upon an altar bright with lights

Where snivelling priests might wish him well-a-day.

Now Neron was a man preoccupied

With the huge spectacle of impotence

Swarming upon an ether-floating planet

Which only people called astronomers

Paused to take any heed of. Other men

Hurried and worried over this and that,

And passed from birth to death in one short eye-wink

Of aching agitation. Fools, parlous fools,

To aged Neron, but a stupendous jest

Fit for the crumpling of old bones in laughter.

Sneering was a capable sort of sport

If one had learnt the trick of balancing

On an impalpable circumference

To whirl a quite detached and sharpened vision

Over inanities a decent planet

Might be ashamed to carry. Neron took

His younger self as motto; every phase

Which others linger in had once been his,

But in the end he had flung clear of all.

They served him in the way of illustration.

He built them up like blocks to knock them down

And chuckle at the noise they made in falling.

These visions of himself were warlock dreams

Conjured up with a wand-stroke from the air

And swept away as easily upon

The imperious order of another gesture.

This pastime lifted Neron to a god,

Or something similar, if only language

Had found a word for it. But superstition

Held words too rigid in a certain groove

For any purpose Neron had for them;

Giving a thing no name exacts obedience

To any chasing colour or humour one

May need to clap to it, and he, at least,

Swam high above convention in his thoughts.

Under the criss-cross beams and chiming bells

Old Neron sat, cheating himself with dreams,

Spreading them out before him, one by one,

As dowagers tap down their playing cards

With claw-like hands in games of solitaire.

His frozen eyes gleamed at them as they came

Out of the darkness from an eldritch past

Which seemed no longer his, yet tasted sweet

In far-off recollection. Childhood first —

But what was childhood? A small, fragile thing

Of gay mishaps, and silly, bootless joys,

An eagerness of folly over tops,

Or kites which tugged and sharply broke their strings

Leaving a heartache Neron chirped to think

No greatest misery could give him now.

Youth bettered this. His jellied blood became

Less solid pondering upon the heat

Which burns youth into powder; his old bones

Were brittle, maybe, but not to that fire,

And yet its simulacrum was most fit

To muse upon and glow vicariously,

Warming safe fingers at a painted flame.

And Neron felt a queasy sort of pride

In mocking his old wounds with jibes that pricked

To a delicious flood of memory.

The hurt outgrown was tonic to his years.

He plied his ridicule so lustily

His body shook and rattled where he sat.

But manhood, flattering itself with windy praise,

Hugging the spiky guerdon of a name

With letters to it, gratified beyond

Desire by the cheap grace of epithet —

What monument of satire was this!

What exquisite lampooning! — O, the mirth

Of stars and ribbons viewed from the vast height

Of Neron's imperturbability!

To chip a quondam purpose to a grin

Was sport to make him hug his pointed knees

And rock for very glee, until his thighs

Were bruised with teetering upon the floor

Whose only cushion was the heaped-up dust.

How good to lick the sauce from all those years

And leave them icy bare and shivering,

With no illusion for their nakedness,

Turned playthings for a man of doting age

Who had no other joy but these, and sleep.

A little sift of daylight wandered in

Where one of the roof-tiles had blown away

And rain and sun had rotted through the wood.

This wisp of light was company to Neron.

He watched the floor-boards change from dark to
          glare,

Saw the glow creep upon a cock of dust

And leave it flat in shadow, traced its course

To where the hole's edge snapped it swiftly off,

Striking him blind to the accustomed dusk.

Now Neron had a friend he never met,

A verger who winked at his being there

In the sky-loft where no one ever came,

And left him scraps of broken meat and bread

Upon a step of the third stairway down.

The light was Neron's clock; it lit a crack

Jagged and strange, not like another crack,

So Neron knew the time. With many a curse

And groan he twitched his shaking bones upright

And tottered down the stair to get his meat,

For he must eat to live and dream his dreams.

He hated it, the aching journey down

And up again, he hated even his bones

Whose insolence in so demanding food

Sent him to get it whatever cost

To old, unable feet and quaking knees;

He loathed the verger's charitable dole,

The need of it became an injury.

But Neron still must eat, and so he went

Wearily down the stair to get his food.

It was not easy eating with the rats

Swarming upon him, but Neron long ago

Had crawled about his loft and gathered in

Such bits of bars, and bolts, and wooden blocks

As workmen leave, and sitting there he shied

These craftily into the horde of rats

And kept them from him while he eat his meat.

And afterwards, filled for more cursing, he

Would fumble round and pick his weapons up,

Treasuring them with canny, careful count

Lest one among the number might be missed,

To serve him for another meal to-morrow.

So the days went, one pea-like to another,

The seasons unremarked, the years a loss.

No Monday, Tuesday, Wednesday were, for Neron,

Just when the light was there and when 'twas not,

With dreams and slumber as each chose to come —

This, he would think, was sure philosophy,

Proper to please the minds of dry old men

Outgrown of creeds and fallals, seeing far

Beyond the hazards itching younger folk

With livelier arteries, whose dumb-bell heads

Were crowned with donkeys' ears. Old bones are wise

And undisturbed by any hum of flesh;

He knew this with a wizened irony.

Weighing the world and life against his bones,

He tipped the scales down heavily, he thought,

And so was satisfied. His cackling laugh

Piped to the rats and hanging spiders' webs

And smothered in the muffle of decay.

The wine of his conceit was very old

And heady; like a drug, it ran beneath

His skin and flushed his veins so that they stood

Out on him like blue worms. A queer old man,

Building content with each new creaking thought

That jarred across his draughty, shrivelled brain.

One day as he was groping in the dusk,

The dusty dusk through which the light-streak clove

And showed it such for some few broomstick lengths,

His startled fingers closed about a foot,

Two feet, in fact, a pair of human feet,

Palpable to his touch, but cold as snow.

Old Neron cringed from them and hid his eyes.

For might he not be going mad? Yes, mad!

That last cold horror haunting vacant age?

His toothless jaws chattered and slabbered now

For one pale moment, then he looked and saw

Two wooden statues in the golden dusk:

A king with orb and sceptre, and a beard

As black as ink, beside him was his queen,

And both were crowned. The beard held Neron's eyes.

Waist-long and vast, its heaviness of hair

Stamped the king's sullen masculinity

With something of grave terror. Neron felt

An instant loathing, tingled with shrewd fear;

And yet, although he shuddered, a sly spark

Of admiration twinged him like a pain.

This was a terrible and virile king.

But for the queen — old Neron gasped before

Her sudden loveliness. A slender plant

Swung in a wind, crowned by a pyramid

Of fragile, jostling bells, was not more like

Itself than she to it. Her eyes were kind,

But wise withal, and hooded with fatigue.

She drooped in standing, yet remained upright

Wistfully conscious of an effort so.

Her pleated robe of green, or blue, or green,

Pushed out or hollowed as her body pressed

Upon it or withdrew within its folds;

She stood as naked to old Neron's eyes

As though no robe were there. Her small white hands

Held a red fox-glove, charming in its poise;

Her feet, which caught the sliding spray of light,

Appeared to tread on gold. Neron beheld

Them, bitter bearded king, mighty in power,

And gentle queen all weariful repose.

The light moved on and Neron saw no more.

Who were they? Neron plagued his memory

For some stray fact he might have heard of them.

But nothing came. He probed a curious mind

Into the reason for their banishment

To this lost corner whence no one had climbed

For desert lengths of years; he did not know

How long he had himself been there, death-long

He thought, and tallied up his distant dreams

As glittering from the other side of life.

Day after day he pondered why so late

He had encountered them. His wisp of light

Fell always to a line; but this was fact

Which baffled speculation. His own dreams

Fogged to a hueless essence, here was more

To work upon; with such a king and queen

Things had moved gaudily — if that were all.

He guessed the word ill-chosen, half a truth,

And seeking the other half, he wrought them both

Into a tale of tragic circumstance,

Of bargained marriage hurried on through lust,

Of desolate surrender where no hope

Of moving iron wills could have a place,

Of girlhood torn upon the state of queen.

With scraps of ancient myths, and fairy-tales,

And half-remembered tags of history,

Neron made up a story his old dreams

Could nowise counter with. He let them be,

Forsaking his life to consider theirs:

The terrible and unrelenting king,

The queen with a red fox-glove in her hands.

So Neron changed the order of his dreams

And irony became magnificence.

The queen, composed and cool, bent to his will,

Moving with stately graciousness within

The frame of his imaginings. She fringed

His dream with filigrees of excellence,

A lace of buds and scarcely opened flowers

Just touched with morning hoar-frost. But the king

Had his own dreams and would not enter Neron's,

Black dreams peculiar to a bearded king.

They injured Neron in his own esteem,

Chafing him to achieve a greater thing

Than he had yet conceived. His ardour grew

To match himself against the king, and crack

The shell of high omnipotence in two

And gloat upon the scattered empty halves

Lolling lopsided on the dusty floor.

So gradually he wrought a miracle,

Merging himself into the royal dream —

But not as ancient Neron, that old man

Had plumped himself with visions of the queen

Into a proper youth whose sap ran hot

Over his gusty body, ripe for love,

Fresh with the bursting agony of love,

And she a very distant, youthful queen.

As long as he could see them, Neron sat

Before the statues, while the light-streak crawled

From king to queen and left them in the dark.

Bit after bit he added to his dream.

He found the castle where they lived, above

A meadow of fair trees, whose flickering leaves

Chequered the placid water of a moat,

Weed-spotted, sound asleep, beneath the walls,

Except when the portcullis, clanging down,

Shattered its sky and trees to sliding planes

Of colour tipping with the tilt of waves.

Above the angry walls was gleam of grass

Shuttled with gold and white, for on a terrace

A peacock strutted between carven shields

Flanking the angles of a balustrade.

Sometimes, at night, Neron would climb the hill,

And crouching down beside the brooding moat

Gaze at the silent glisten of the roof

And ivy-twinkling walls, and speculate

Which hollow window opened on the room

Where the queen slept, and curse the bearded king

With full-mouthed curses. Then, as dreaming grew,

He saw the queen at work within her bower

Surrounded by her ladies, stitching on

A blue-green tapestry where hunters ran,

And spotted dogs plunged into a blue stream

After an otter. Neron boldly stepped

Into the bower and nodded to the ladies

Who crept away and left him with the queen.

But nothing happened, for that night the king came,

Though Neron luckily escaped before.

He wrenched his wits to find some casual way

When he might urge himself upon her thought

Whose numb inconsequence was salt and flame

Set to the green wound of his smarting flesh.

But the dream halted at this very spot,

He could not push it to a consummation.

He heaved upon it with his new-found strength,

Fully persuaded that he served her cause

By this he had in mind. The dream gave way,

The queen surrendered on the very terrace

Where the white peacock strutted. She whispered Neron

Where she would be at sunset, gave him the key

Of a small turret-chamber. He found her there,

Her slender shadow stretching to the door

To welcome him; and she, beyond her shadow,

Stood waiting in the crimson sunset light,

A slender silver fox-glove flushed with rose.

There was no sound except the golden boom

Of bees among the honeysuckle flowers

Stirring against the wall. For neither spoke,

Being removed past any reach of speech

Into that silent space of holiness

Where flesh creates the everlasting world.

But there the bearded king broke in upon them,

The king whose dream would never enter Neron's.

When Neron saw that thorny face, he leapt

To hide it from the queen. Calling his dream,

He strode upon the king, and the dream followed

Inch by inch after him, close as a shadow.

But Neron's dream was mighty with fulfilment,

It strove with the king's dream, and he and Neron

Stood each beside his dream and urged it forward

With shouts and cries. The battle roared between
            them.

The king's dream crowded down on Neron's dream

To smother it. But Neron's dream arose,

Flinging the king's dream off, and towered up

Tremendous in its brilliance. Then the king,

To save his dream, threw his black beard upon it,

The heaviness of hair shut out the brilliance,

At which his dream, revived to fearful fury,

Came on at Neron's dream, and the two clashed
With a great noise together, and their bodies
Rang each on each like cymbals in the gloom
Sprung suddenly about them. With the dark,
The king's dream waxed monstrous in shape and stat-
    ure,
Behemoth treading on a puny earth,
So did it stand and move, a ponderous bulk,
The nimbleness of Neron's dream was nothing.
The king's dream lifted like a rock and drove
The air snarling before it to a height
Past vision, thence it fell on Neron's dream,
Splitting its back from end to end, and Neron
Waggled his palsied hands about and wept.

The verger, coming up with Neron's food,
Found what was left the day before untouched.
But being somewhat slow of wit, indeed
A person of marked unagility

Where thinking was concerned, what speculations

Another might have had, he was without.

So laying the second dole beside the first

He stumped downstairs to dust the chancel rail.

But when, next day, two baskets greeted him,

Both full, he felt enough perplexity

To risk a whistle on it; and the third

Encounter with the baskets, all of them,

Induced such lively wonder that he climbed

The three long flights of curling stairs to see

What ailed old Neron. Scratching match on match

He came at last upon him, crushed beneath

A fallen wooden statue, dead as nails.

"The poor old beggar was dead as last year's fly,"

He told his mates, and later told the Dean,

And also mentioned something of a figure

Of painted wood. And there were two of them,

A king and queen, so wondrously preserved

They looked quite new, although the architect

Pronounced them very early specimens

Of thirteenth century work, at which the Dean

And Chapter all said "Ah!" and spent a week

Searching old records for a hint of them.

The local antiquaries blew the dust

From ancient chronicles and seared their eyes

With cryptic script to learn what history

Made mention of an inky-bearded king

Whose iron mien portended fearful things,

And who the queen, so obviously mismated?

But not a dusty chronicle gave tongue.

Baffled, they placed them in the town museum

Cautiously labelled, "Ancient King and Queen,

Fine specimens of Thirteenth Century Carving."

And what of Neron? Neron was a pauper,

They buried him, of course, in Potter's Field,

Where you can see him turned to purple thistles

Purveying exquisite delight to donkeys

On Sundays, holidays, and festivals,

When the white sky is filled with hallelujahs

Profusely scattered by Cathedral bells.

THE SISTERS

TAKING us by and large, we're a queer lot
We women who write poetry. And when you think
How few of us there've been, it's queerer still.
I wonder what it is that makes us do it,
Singles us out to scribble down, man-wise,
The fragments of ourselves. Why are we
Already mother-creatures, double-bearing,
With matrices in body and in brain?
I rather think that there is just the reason
We are so sparse a kind of human being;
The strength of forty thousand Atlases
Is needed for our every-day concerns.
There's Sapho, now I wonder what was Sapho.
I know a single slender thing about her:
That, loving, she was like a burning birch-tree

All tall and glittering fire, and that she wrote

Like the same fire caught up to Heaven and held
     there,

A frozen blaze before it broke and fell.

Ah, me! I wish I could have talked to Sapho,

Surprised her reticences by flinging mine

Into the wind. This tossing off of garments

Which cloud the soul is none too easy doing

With us to-day. But still I think with Sapho

One might accomplish it, were she in the mood

To bare her loveliness of words and tell

The reasons, as she possibly conceived them,

Of why they are so lovely. Just to know

How she came at them, just to watch

The crisp sea sunshine playing on her hair,

And listen, thinking all the while 'twas she

Who spoke and that we two were sisters

Of a strange, isolated little family.

And she is Sapho — Sapho — not Miss or Mrs.,

A leaping fire we call so for convenience;

But Mrs. Browning — who would ever think

Of such presumption as to call her "Ba."

Which draws the perfect line between sea-cliffs

And a close-shuttered room in Wimpole Street.

Sapho could fly her impulses like bright

Balloons tip-tilting to a morning air

And write about it. Mrs. Browning's heart

Was squeezed in stiff conventions. So she lay

Stretched out upon a sofa, reading Greek

And speculating, as I must suppose,

In just this way on Sapho; all the need,

The huge, imperious need of loving, crushed

Within the body she believed so sick.

And it was sick, poor lady, because words

Are merely simulacra after deeds

Have wrought a pattern; when they take the place

Of actions they breed a poisonous miasma

Which, though it leave the brain, eats up the body.

So Mrs. Browning, aloof and delicate,

Lay still upon her sofa, all her strength

Going to uphold her over-topping brain.

It seems miraculous, but she escaped

To freedom and another motherhood

Than that of poems. She was a very woman

And needed both.

        If I had gone to call,

Would Wimpole Street have been the kindlier place,

Or Casa Guidi, in which to have met her?

I am a little doubtful of that meeting,

For Queen Victoria was very young and strong

And all-pervading in her apogee

At just that time. It we had stuck to poetry,

Sternly refusing to be drawn off by mesmerism

Or Roman revolutions, it might have done.

For, after all, she is another sister,

But always, I rather think, an older sister

And not herself so curious a technician

As to admit newfangled modes of writing —

"Except, of course, in Robert, and that is neither

Here nor there for Robert is a genius."

I do not like the turn this dream is taking,

Since I am very fond of Mrs. Browning

And very much indeed should like to hear her

Graciously asking me to call her "Ba."

But then the Devil of Verisimilitude

Creeps in and forces me to know she wouldn't.

Convention again, and how it chafes my nerves,

For we are such a little family

Of singing sisters, and as if I didn't know

What those years felt like tied down to the sofa.

Confound Victoria, and the slimy inhibitions

She loosed on all us Anglo-Saxon creatures!

Suppose there hadn't been a Robert Browning,

No "Sonnets from the Portuguese" would have been
    written.

They are the first of all her poems to be,

One might say, fertilized. For, after all,

A poet is flesh and blood as well as brain

And Mrs. Browning, as I said before,

Was very, very woman. Well, there are two

Of us, and vastly unlike that's for certain.

Unlike at least until we tear the veils

Away which commonly gird souls. I scarcely think

Mrs. Browning would have approved the process

In spite of what had surely been relief;

For speaking souls must always want to speak

Even when bat-eyed, narrow-minded Queens

Set prudishness to keep the keys of impulse.

Then do the frowning Gods invent new banes

And make the need of sofas. But Sapho was dead

And I, and others, not yet peeped above

The edge of possibility. So that's an end

To speculating over tea-time talks

Beyond the movement of pentameters

With Mrs. Browning.

But I go dreaming on,

In love with these my spiritual relations.

I rather think I see myself walk up

A flight of wooden steps and ring a bell

And send a card in to Miss Dickinson.

Yet that's a very silly way to do.

I should have taken the dream twist-ends about

And climbed over the fence and found her deep

Engrossed in the doings of a humming-bird

Among nasturtiums. Not having expected strangers,

She might forget to think me one, and holding up

A finger say quite casually: "Take care.

Don't frighten him, he's only just begun."

"Now this," I well believe I should have thought,

"Is even better than Sapho. With Emily

You're really here, or never anywhere at all

In range of mind." Wherefore, having begun

In the strict centre, we could slowly progress

To various circumferences, as we pleased.

We could, but should we? That would quite depend

On Emily. I think she'd be exacting,

Without intention possibly, and ask

A thousand tight-rope tricks of understanding.

But, bless you, I would somersault all day

If by so doing I might stay with her.

I hardly think that we should mention souls

Although they might just round the corner from us

In some half-quizzical, half-wistful metaphor.

I'm very sure that I should never seek

To turn her parables to stated fact.

Sapho would speak, I think, quite openly,

And Mrs. Browning guard a careful silence,

But Emily would set doors ajar and slam them

And love you for your speed of observation.

Strange trio of my sisters, most diverse,

And how extraordinarily unlike

Each is to me, and which way shall I go?

Sapho spent and gained; and Mrs. Browning,

After a miser girlhood, cut the strings

Which tied her money-bags and let them run;

But Emily hoarded — hoarded — only giving

Herself to cold, white paper. Starved and tortured,

She cheated her despair with games of patience

And fooled herself by winning. Frail little elf,

The lonely brain-child of a gaunt maturity,

She hung her womanhood upon a bough

And played ball with the stars — too long — too

    long —

The garment of herself hung on a tree

Until at last she lost even the desire

To take it down. Whose fault? Why let us say,

To be consistent, Queen Victoria's.

But really, not to over-rate the queen,

I feel obliged to mention Martin Luther,

And behind him the long line of Church Fathers

Who draped their prurience like a dirty cloth

About the naked majesty of God.

Good-bye, my sisters, all of you are great,

And all of you are marvellously strange,

And none of you has any word for me.

I cannot write like you, I cannot think

In terms of Pagan or of Christian now.

I only hope that possibly some day

Some other woman with an itch for writing

May turn to me as I have turned to you

And chat with me a brief few minutes. How

We lie, we poets! It is three good hours

I have been dreaming. Has it seemed so long

To you? And yet I thank you for the time

Although you leave me sad and self-distrustful,

For older sisters are very sobering things.

Put on your cloaks, my dears, the motor's waiting.

No, you have not seemed strange to me, but near,

Frightfully near, and rather terrifying.

I understand you all, for in myself —

Is that presumption? Yet indeed it's true —

We are one family. And still my answer

Will not be any one of yours, I see.

Well, never mind that now. Good night! Good night!

VIEW OF TEIGNMOUTH IN
DEVONSHIRE

*"Atkins the coachman, Bartlett the surgeon, and the Girls over
at the Bonnet-shop, say we shall now have a month of seasonable
weather — warm, witty, and full of invention."*
            Letter from Keats to Reynolds. March 14, 1818.

IT's a soppy, splashy, muddy country

And he is dead sick of stair and entry,

Of four walls cuddling round his chair,

And breathing full as much water as air.

London is so far away

It dreams, like Latmos. He has sat all day

Copying that cursed Fourth Book and he's struck

A snag, and his drying sand won't suck.

His mind's like a seed gone to rot with rain,

And — Damn it, there's poor Tom coughing again!

Mr. John Keats crams his hat well on

Over his ears and walks up and down

The soggy streets of Teignmouth town.

Mr. John Keats walks along the streets

Of Teignmouth and asks every soul he meets

If the sun ever shines in Devonshire,

Whether the weather they live with here

Is sometimes what one might really call fair,

With the sun in the sky and a brisk to the air?

The hat of Mr. John Keats is wet,

But his eyes are sharp and ferret-set,

He is seeking the sun with a quicksilver-rod,

Noting the veer in a neighbour's nod,

Gauging the drift of a neighbour's words

As they might be a flock of South-come birds.

Atkins, the coachman, sets his mug

Down on the counter and gives a shrug.

"Lor' love you, Sir, if I was to tell

The way I know, you might call it smell.

I smell it right across the rain,

Dry and gentle; it's plain as plain

To-day, I give it a week to run,

This rain, and then we'll have the sun,

As skittish as a piebald colt

And sudden as a thunderbolt.

All full o' notions, that's the way

Of the sun down here on a Summer's day.

Just take my word, before you've said

'Jack Robinson,' you'll be hugging the shade

Of every wall, and sweatin' in

A steam like my team when I bring 'em in.

Well, thank ye, Sir, I don't mind if I do,

Brandy neat is my usual brew."

Smell it, could he? The man's insane.

Smell the sun through a week of rain!

Yet the thought has a kind of glamour to it,

A relish of wit, however you view it,

A rainbow quip for a rainy day.

Mr. Keats, plodding through wet clay,

Is aware of a certain direct effect

Of joy in his heart. He stands erect.

Surely the mist is silvering

His footsteps sound with a livelier ring.

If anything glitters in Teignmouth streets

This afternoon, it is John Keats.

Mr. Bartlett is hurrying by

At a speed which announces that minutes fly,

But he pauses briefly just to say

"Ah, Mr. Keats, how are you to-day?

The sun? Oh, very shortly now.

We shall be scorched before we know.

Didn't you hear the crows this morning?

They always give one plenty of warning.

And Mrs. Bartlett talks of house-cleaning,

Every married man can read the meaning

Of that. When the women begin to clack

It's a surer sign than the almanac.

The barometer's risen a point or two

Since yesterday, and this mist is blue,

Not grey. I am sorry I cannot stop,

But a surgeon is always on the hop,

If it's not for one thing, it's another.

Of course you're anxious because of your brother.

Tell him he'll soon have all the basking

In sunlight he wants, and just for the asking.

But I must go, Mrs. Green's brought to bed —

Oh, tell him to keep it off of his head."

Smash! Bang! Mr. Keats. Another chain

Is snapped, and there's a gold tint to the rain.

Simmons the barber's as shrunk as a pippin

Hung on a beam which you might nick a chip in,

But never could suck for its juice is all dried.

This afternoon he is standing inside

His doorway, just behind his pole,

With the mien of a migratory soul

Perching an instant before departing

Otherwhere, he seems always just starting

To leave, a whirling weather-cock

On the edge of flight, but tied to a block.

"Good afternoon, Mr. Keats," says he,

"Brushing up a bit for good weather, I see.

That's the way, young men can tell

A season's turn uncommonly well.

I've had a full day, the whole town at once.

But when I learnt my trade every dunce

Who could snap a scissors did not dare hoist a pole.

I remember one day when they called out the roll

In the old sixty-third, every man of the lot

Was new shaved and powdered and wound, and my pot

And razors all cleaned and I with the rest of them

As spick and as span I could match with the best of
     them.

To cut a round head requires some skill,

But nothing to binding a cue, there's a thrill

In a nicely tied cue, I can't see how the girls

Can put up with a man who wears his own curls.

But fashion is fashion, the hussy, and I've

Been her very devoted since I've been alive.

And, thank God, she has not yet set her approval

On beards except in the way of removal.

I wish you could feel the delight I receive

When my razor slides over your skin, I'd as leave

Shave a man in his twenties as go to a play,

There's romance in it, Sir, when you see the soap
    spray

Into bubbles and lather, and your blade cuts a line

And lets through the smooth face like a moon, it's so
    fine

That I dream it sometimes. I've a soul for such fan-
    cies,

Old barbers like shaving as young girls like dances.

And one makes the other. Who would dance a quad-
    rille
With a rough, stubble chin? That fellow who will
Is a hater of women, a thief in the egg,
He's just ripe for a ball attached to his leg.
Why look, Sir, and tell me if fully two-thirds
Of the unshaven men do not end as jail-birds.
Our prisons are full of them, I dare to swear
No convict's without a two-days' growth of hair.
I don't hold with this personal shaving, it's sordid.
A man should spend well on himself, I wish more did.
But no man can cut his own hair, that's a fact,
And a hair-cut requires a vast deal of tact.
A doctor wants his to look sober and grave,
Tradesmen are addicted to a float and a wave,
And again, one must know the sort of commodity
Your client purveys or there's danger of oddity.
A butcher cut like a silk-mercer won't do.
And a military man must carry a clue

To his martial exploits in the style of his head,

While a poet — you're a poet, Sir, I think I've heard
     said —

Oh, no, Sir, indeed, not a bit more confined,

A poet's hair should seem the least trifle inclined

To a graceful disorder, it should look well when tossed;

If you cut it too short this effect is quite lost.

Oh, I beg, Mr. Keats, not another least snip.

Oh, dear, I do really regret that last clip.

I am glad you are pleased, but I don't think a poet

Should order his hair so that no one can know it.

Still, you look very well, though I should have pre-
     ferred

More dash and confusion for you. I have heard

That Lord Byron measures his hair with a rule

Before it is cut, and the least thimbleful

Too much taken off sets him all in a taking.

I've been told of men who couldn't cut him for shak-
     ing.

The weather will change in less than a week,
I have felt it these last few days on my cheek,
My skin always answers to the slightest degree
Of more or less moisture. You'll hardly agree
That it's dryer and warmer, but my touch is so fine
I can tell a South wind when it's over the line.
Of course they'll say different, these poor rustic
      churls,
But you be all ready for sparking the girls
By Tuesday. I'll tip you the wink. We old men
Remember our own young days, now and again."

Mr. John Keats has a jaunty swing
In his gait, as he leaves the chattering
Old barber, bowing beside his door.
Of course he feels the sort of core
Of golden sun the mist falls through.
What is a day, what is two?
The sun is coming up from the line

Like a fifty-four with its sails ashine.

He feels the flower-scented South

Like a taste of apricot in his mouth.

He thinks of primroses under the hedge

Where the pathway runs by the sheer cliff edge;

Of the downs above where sheep have trod

Crooked grey patterns across the sod,

And the shadows of turf-walls, cool and still,

Mark who owns where all down the hill;

Of a long slow ocean, so dazzling bright

Its blue is smothered in spangled white.

He thinks of queer sea-paths cross-running,

Smooth on ripple, of the quiet sunning

Of rocks and meadows, of violets

Creeping through grass, of drying nets,

Of poetry read with the sun on his book

And the freckling of leaves for an overlook.

Somebody laughs, somebody calls,

"Good-day, Mr. Keats." It drops from the walls,

A perfume of laughter which flutters and falls.

Lime-tree blossoms by turret stairs,

Laughter of flowers no more than theirs,

Sunny golden acacia blooms

Peeping into maidens' rooms,

Snap a spray and throw it over

The window-ledge to a waiting lover.

Mr. Keats comes to a stop

For the girls are over the Bonnet-shop

Leaning out like waving roses

Over a gate, most lovely of poses.

"Stay where you are, Girls," says Mr. Keats,

"You pose as the dryads of Teignmouth streets.

If Haydon were here he would jot you down

In a jiffy, with your hair wet and blown

And your little laughing faces like pansies."

"La! Mr. Keats, you do have such fancies."

"Fancies or no, I believe it clears.

Don't you feel the sun on your cheeks, my Dears?

Or smell it perhaps? What do you think?

There's a hocus-pocus to-day in my ink

Which would not let me write a line,

And I itch for the sight of a columbine.

Tell me, have you noticed anything

Which points to a near-by Summering?"

"Oh yes," said little Number One,

"All day I have felt the sun,

I saw it on a wheat-straw bonnet

I was making, the sun lay upon it,

And I thought the muslin blue-bells were sweet.'

"That," said Mr. Keats, "is proof complete."

Said Number Two, "I pricked my thumb

Three times running, and fair days come

After three pricks, it is always so.

Grandmother taught me long ago."

"I dreamt last night," said Number Three,

"Of a great thick-leaved fuchsia-tree

Full of blossoms, purple and red,

And the blossoms played music over my head

Like bells of glass and copper bells

And wind in the trees when the ocean swells

Flood tide over the beach, and shells

Glisten like rubies with the water sheen

And the sky at the back of the town is green."

"You prophesy in a parable,"

Said Mr. Keats. "Oh, April-fool!"

Cried the girls who were over the Bonnet-shop.

And their laughter was sweet as a lollipop

To an urchin's palate in his ears.

With a gesture, he brushed aside their jeers.

"But will it clear?" "Of course it will,"

Said the three, "if you patiently wait until

It does." And they laughed in a rainbow chord,

High, and low, and middleward.

And Mr. Keats laughed too, though he knew

That they had not said one word in two

Of what he'd imagined they might have said.

But who cares a button who bakes the bread

So the bread is baked? And a Bonnet-shop

May be what you please, even Latmos top.

So Mr. Keats went blithely on,

Quite as if the round sun shone,

Back to his copying his Fourth Book.

And the girls watched him until a crook

In the street, when he turned it, hid him from sight.

Then they noticed that it was growing night.

So they put their bonnets away, and the three

Lit the lamp and sat down to tea,

Immortal for always, because John Keats

Had taken a walk through Teignmouth streets,

And stopped when one of them said "Good-day."

Clio is odd in her ways, they say.

The coachman, the surgeon, the barber, the girls —

Islands raised out of darkening swirls.

Who else was in Teignmouth that afternoon?

Vainly may we importune

The shadows, only these have come down

A century from Teignmouth town.

These only from the dark are won

Because John Keats had a hunger for sun.

FOOL O' THE MOON

THE silver-slippered moon treads the blue tiles of the
    sky,
And I
See her dressed in golden roses,
With a single breast uncovered,
The carnation tip of it
Urgent for a lover's lip.
So she dances to a stately
Beat, with poses most sedately
Taken, yet there lies
Something wanton in her gestures,
And there is surprise of coquetry
In the falling of her vestures.
Why?

Out of old mythology,

With a pulse of gourds and sheep-skins,

Banging bronze and metal thunders,

There is she,

Wonderfullest of earth's wonders.

As for me,

Head thrown back and arms spread wide

Like a zany crucified,

I stand watching, waiting, gazing,

All of me spent in amazing,

Longing for her wheat-white thighs,

Thirsting for her emerald fire,

My desire

Pounding dully from my eyes.

And my hands

Clutch and cuddle the vast air

Seeking her where she's most fair.

There,

On the cool blue tiles of heaven,

She is dancing coolly, coldly,

Footsteps trace a braid of seven,

And her gauzy garments fleet

Round her like a glittering sleet.

Suddenly she flings them boldly

In a streaming bannerall

Out behind,

And I see all.

God! I'm blind!

And a goodly company

Of men are we,

Lovers she has chosen,

Laughing-stocks and finger-posts

To the wise, a troupe of ghosts

Swelled by every century.

Mad, and blind, and burnt, and frozen,

Standing on a hilly slope

At bright midnight,

And our hope

Is in vain, or is it not?

Legend knows the very spot

Where the moon once made her bed.

But the pathway as it led

Over rock-brows to that valley

Is an alley choked and dead.

One by one our fates deceive us,

One of hundreds will be shown

Ferny uplands whose great bosses

Of tall granite hide the mosses

Where our Lady's lying prone,

All her stars withdrawn, alone.

So she chooses to receive us,

Out of hundreds, only one.

Such a vale of moss and heather

Spreads about us, hither — thither.

Hush!

Shall I tell what befell

Once behind that bush.

When the rattling pods at noon

Made a music in September.

Shall I say what I remember —

While the long, sea-grasses croon,

And the sea-spray on the sand

Chips the silence from the land?

Hush, then, let me say it soon.

I have lain with Mistress Moon.

TOMB VALLEY

Down a cliff-side where rock-roses,
Shallow-rooted, scantly bloom,
And the mountain goats in passing
Barely find a foothold's room,
While the boulders of the summit
Cast an everlasting gloom.

Leaps a torrent from behind
The jutted angle of a wall
In a long, unbroken sliding,
For it touches not at all
Any rock, or stone, or pebble
For a thousand feet of fall.

For a thousand feet it rushes
Like a heavy, laden air,

Playing over some tremendous
Sound which surely must be there,
For you hear it, lose it, hear it.
Does it come from anywhere?

Seething, bubbling, churning, groaning,
Has the water in its flight
Shattered on the stony bottom
Of the valley, while its height
Drawing upward like a ribbon
Palely grows upon the sight?

But the sound is chiller, deeper,
Long and dreary like a moan
Caught forever on an echo
'Twixt two balanced shafts of stone,
Whence it surges and resurges
In protracted monotone.

Far below, within the valley,

Runs a river, cold and sleek,

Never oar has cut its smoothness,

It has shattered on no beak

Of shallop or of galley,

Its tide is slow and meek.

And the trees within that valley,

Of every broad-leaved kind,

Wave to and fro compactly,

For there's never any wind.

Ten thousand branches blowing

All one way is hard to find.

And the shadows which their movement

Casts upon the sandy ground

Are like footsteps weaving dances

To that ghastly, haunting sound

Ringing round the chilly valley,

Round and round and round and round.

Where the river curves about it,

And the water lilies strew

Silver petals on the pebbles

Mingling with dropped cones of yew,

Stands a sepulchre of granite

Striped with bars of green and blue.

Green and blue bars painted crosswise

From its bottom to its crown,

At its apex is a statue,

Coldly, boldly, gazing down,

Gazing fiercely, gazing wildly,

In an everlasting frown.

And upon its knees a woman

Kneels and clasps the granite thighs,

And clings upon the roughened stone
While tears drop from her eyes.
The surly yews wave back and forth
Beneath a red moonrise.

And a hollow, draughty moaning
Fills the valley like a gong.
Women's voices weeping, wailing,
All the waving trees among,
Where no shapes or shadows flicker
But the low moon, broad and long.

Slowly rising from the cliff-tops,
Like a gnawed and crumbled cone,
It appears in perfect semblance
To a sepulchre of stone,
And the bars are striped upon it
Like cross-sticks of blackened bone.

In a bitter orange moonlight
Lies the woman on the knees
Of that austere thing of granite,
All surrounded by the trees,
And the curling, sneering river,
And nothing else but these.

On a sudden, she has risen,
And with clenched fists beats the face
Of that frozen granite horror,
And her blows in that drear place
Are as thunder-claps resounding
Upon vastnesses of space.

For an instant still she batters
At that changeless, mocking frown,
Then flings her bleeding hands
Above her head and plunges down

To the smooth and careful river
With sere rushes overgrown.

But no ripple marks her entrance
To that water, bright as flame,
And no pucker stirs the granite face
To tell she ever came.
The trees blow and the moaning
Continues just the same.

But every moonlight night, they say,
She drowns herself once more,
And by the queasy daylight
You can see her from the shore
Lying like a lily petal
On the river's glassy floor.

So they say, but no one proves it.
No one ever ventures in

To that valley. Only passers-by

Above can hear a thin

Weary wailing, if they note it

Through the torrent's distant din.

As they wander on the cliff-edge

Where the scant rock-roses blow,

And the mountain goats go shrewdly

In the footways that they know,

While the crash of tumbling water

Sounds a thousand feet below.

THE GREEN PARRAKEET

"THREE doors up from the end of the street
  Hung a golden cage with a green parrakeet."
His feet shambled in the dust of the road, and the
  little barberry bushes hung out red tongues and
  leered at him.
He shuffled on, down the road, bent as though it might
  be a load he was carrying, while tiers and tiers
  of poplars, birches, hemlocks, pines, peered to
  see who it might be who stumbled and flung the
  dust about,
And the grey grape-vines, in and out between the
  bushes, ran beside him and looked in his face.
But his pace never changed a whit for all their staring.
  He shuffled on at his long way-faring.

"Morning and night, to the green parrakeet
She sang, and Oh, her singing was sweet!"
The road dipped down to a marsh, and the mea-
dow-larks sang as he passed them, but his ears
rang with another singing so that he heard nothing.

"By the North Wind's whistle, he is blind!" said a
moose-wood to an elder-bush.

"Hush," cried the grape-vines, "you do not catch his
dust. It is the dust of something a long way off."

"Her kisses were a flower red;
I saw them on the bird's green head.
Her breasts were white as almond bean
And the parrakeet nestled in between."
"Oh, gently, gently," sighed the sentimental vines,
but the long lines of trees behind them objected
that he took a great while to go by.

"We are better employed," they declared, "contem-

plating the sky."

Then I knocked at the door and entered in

Like the orange flame of a hidden sin.

I stood before her and there were three —

The parrakeet and I and she.

I tossed her arms apart and pressed

Myself upon her, breast to breast,

And the parrakeet was my bidden guest.

I forced her lips till they caught on mine,

And poured myself down her throat like wine.

I mingled with her, part for part,

But the parrakeet lay next her heart.

Oh, sweeter than her lips were sweet

Was my utter hate for that parrakeet.

She fell from me like the withered shell

Of a cranberry, and it was well;

I stood on the other side of Hell.

Slowly, slowly, she raised her head,

But the parrakeet fell down like lead

Upon the matting, still and dead.

Softly, softly, she gazed at me,

And I saw a thing which I dared not see.

"My love!" she said, and the tones were sweet

As ever she used to the parrakeet.

But I had made my flaming breast

A weapon to kill a bird on its nest —

A single flame for the bird and me,

And I was as smothered as he could be.

I stared at her from the farther side

Of Hell, no space is great beside

This space. I could not see her face

Across such vastitude of space,

And over it drowsed a darkened thing:

A monster parrakeet's green wing.

The air was starred with parrakeets.

I turned and rushed into the streets.

For days and days I wandered there,

For Oh! My love was very fair!

Each night I watched her lean and stand,

With empty heart and empty hand,

While every passer-by she scanned.

But I beheld what was not meet

For all to see — a parrakeet

Of gauzy substance which could cast

No slightest shadow where it passed,

Fluttering with indecent glee

Between my hungering love and me.

Ten months went by, and then one day

It struck my face and flew away.

Some odd obedience in my feet

Compelled me after, street by street,

And then along a country lane.

I had no power to turn again.

Next morning took me farther still,

My feet usurped the place of will.

And now I walk a weary road,

Bent double underneath the load

Of memory and second sight.

That bird is always on my right

And just ahead, I follow where

His body flickers through the air.

Sometimes it is as plain as print,

Sometimes no better than a hint

Of colour where no leaves are green.

But I can see what I have seen.

How many years is that ago?

I notice night and morning flow

Each into each, the seasons run

Against the turning of the sun,

But more or fewer — 'tis all one.

She may be dead, and I may be

A ghost myself, eternally

Dreaming the short, ironic bliss

Of one long, unrepeated kiss.

The man scuffed across a bridge and up a steep hill.
"Quietly, quietly," whispered the barberry-
bushes, and hid their scarlet tongues under the
leaves. "Weep, Tree-Brothers," said the grape-
vines. But the long lines of trees only rustled and
played hide and seek with the peeping moon.
They were too tall to pay much heed to anything
so small as an old man limping up a hill.

TIME'S ACRE

BEAT, beat, with your soft, grey feet,
Tear at the cold, rough stone.
His grave is here, but it's many a year
Since the grass on it was mown.

His ears are crumbled to bitter dust,
His eyes are a hollow bone.
Your twisting hair is bright and fair,
But he is under a stone.

Go back again to your own wide tomb,
Leave him in peace within
His grave that is narrow and shallow and small,
There is no room for two between either wall,
And the walls are caving in.

There are nests of worms in the underground,
And the grass-roots wind across,
Like a counterpane to keep out the rain
Is the green-eyed, clutching moss.

Go back to your tomb a mile away,
Go back through the still bronze door.
The arms which are carven upon its front
Are there as they were before.

No trace of escutcheon is on this stone,
And burdocks have pushed it awry,
And the flowers on tiptoe out of his mouth
Are staring into the sky.

Over his grave is a moan of wind,
And hemlock-trees bow down,
And a hemlock cone lies on the stone

Stained with smoke from the town.

What have you to do in this dismal place
By a dingy, broken stone?
He has no hands and he has no face,
And bone cannot wed with bone.

You took his flesh and you took his heart,
But his bones are his own to keep.
Knuckle and straight, he has them all
Down in the gravel deep.

Perhaps he laughs with his hard grey mouth,
Perhaps he shouts with glee,
And cuddles his bones up one by one,
And wishes that you could see.

Perhaps he plays jackstones with his bones,
And bets how long you will stay.

He knows all about those bright bronze doors
Waiting a mile away.

For you in the flesh teased him in the flesh
And would not let him be,
Till you teased him out of his flesh for good
And into Eternity.

But what is fire to a living man
Is nothing at all to a bone.
He lies at ease in the cold and the mold,
And he lies at ease alone.

He will be part of the earth in time,
You will be only dust,
And your carven door will be nothing more
Than a heap of eating rust.

So much for your azure fleur-de-lis,

And your cross in a chevron d'or.

He will be lilies in a morning breeze

At the foot of a sycamore.

The world goes round, and the world goes round,

And who knows what may come out of the ground

When a man is planted under a mound.

SULTRY

To those who can see them, there are eyes,

Leopard eyes of marigolds crouching above red earth,

Bulging eyes of fruits and rubies in the heavily-
      hanging trees,

Broken eyes of queasy cupids staring from the gloom
      of myrtles.

I came here for solitude

And I am plucked at by a host of eyes.

A peacock spreads his tail on the balustrade

And every eye is a mood of green malice,

A challenge and a fear.

A hornet flashes above geraniums,

Spying upon me in a trick of cunning.

And Hermes,

Hermes the implacable,

Points at me with a fractured arm.

Vengeful god of smooth, imperishable loveliness,

You are more savage than the goat-legged Pan,

Than the crocodile of carven yew-wood.

Fisherman of men's eyes,

You catch them on a three-pronged spear:

Your youth, your manhood,

The reticence of your everlasting revelation.

I too am become a cunning eye

Seeking you past your time-gnawed surface,

Seeking you back to hyacinths upon a dropping hill,

Where legend drowses in a glaze of sea.

Yours are the eyes of a bull and a panther,

For all that they are chiselled out and the sockets
    empty.

You — perfectly imperfect,

Clothed in a garden,

In innumerable gardens,

Borrowing the eyes of fruits and flowers —

And mine also, cold, impossible god,

So that I stare back at myself

And see myself with loathing.

A quince-tree flings a crooked shadow —

My shadow, tortured out of semblance,

Bewildered in quince boughs.

His shadow is clear as a scissored silhouette.

Heat twinkles and the eyes glare.

And I, of the mingled shadow,

I glare

And see nothing.

THE ENCHANTED CASTLE

TO EDGAR ALLAN POE

OLD crumbling stones set long ago upon
The naked headland of a suave green shore.
Old stones all riven into cracks and glands
By moss and ivy. Up above, a peak
Of narrow, iron windows, a hooded tower
With frozen windows looking to the West.
When the sun sets, a winking, fiery light
Riffles the window-panes above the gloom
Of purple waters heaving evenly,
Waters moving about the naked headland
In sombre slowness, with no dash of spray
To strike the stagnant pools and flash the weeds.
                              A rack of shifting clouds
Darkens the waters' margin. On the shore

Are clusters of great trees whose brittle leaves

Crackle together as the mournful wind

Takes them and shakes them. But the tower windows

Fling bloody streams of light across the dusk,

Planges of bloody light which the upper sky

Has hurled at them and now is drawing back.

Behind the tower, where no windows are,

A little wisp of moon catches the stones

So that they glitter palely from the shore,

The suave green shore with all its leaden trees.

AUTUMN AND DEATH

THEY are coy, these sisters, Autumn and Death,
And they both have learnt what it is to wait.
Not a leaf is jarred by their cautious breath,
The little feather-weight
Petals of climbing convolvulus
Are scarcely even tremulous.

Who hears Autumn moving down
The garden-paths? Who marks her head
Above the oat-sheaves? A leaf gone brown
On the ash, and a maple-leaf turned red —
Yet a rose that's freshly blown
Seals your eyes to the change in these,
For it's mostly green about the trees.

And Death with her silver-slippered feet,
Do you hear her walk by your garden-chair?
The cool of her hand makes a tempered heat,
That's all, and the shadow of her hair
Is curiously sweet.
Does she speak? If so, you have not heard;
The whisper of Death is without a word.

The sisters, Autumn and Death, with strange
Long silences, they bide their time,
Nor ever step beyond the range
Allotted to a pantomime.
But the soundless hours chime,
One after one, and their faces grow
To an altered likeness, slow — slow.

Grim is the face which Autumn turns
To a sky all bare of obscuring leaves,

And her hair is red as a torch where it burns

In the dry hearts of the oaten sheaves.

But Death has a face which yearns

With a gaunt desire upon its prey,

And Death's dark face hides yesterday.

Then Autumn holds her hands to touch

Death's hands, and the two kiss, cheek by cheek,

And one smiles to the other, and the smiles say much,

And neither one has need to speak.

Two gray old sisters, such

Are Autumn and Death when their tasks are done,

And their world is a world where a blackened sun

Shines like ebony over the floes

Of a shadeless ice, and no wind blows.

FOLIE DE MINUIT

No word, no word, O Lord God!
Hanging above the shivering pillars
Like thunder over a brazen city.

Pity? Is there pity?
Does pity pour from the multiform points
Of snow crystals?
If the throats of the organ pipes
Are numb with cold,
Can the boldest bellows' blast
Melt their now dumb hosannas?

No word, august and brooding God!
No shrivelled spectre of an aching tone
Can pierce those banners

Which hide your face, your hands,

Your feet at whose slight tread

Frore water curds to freckled sands

Seaweed encrusted.

The organ loft is draughty with faint voices

Weeping,

Which are not mine, nor would be.

I purposed anthems, copper-red and golden,

Thrusting to the hearts of Babylonian Kings,

Bowed down before Judea and its Highest,

That God of Hosts who screens himself with ban-
    ners.

My finger-tips are cast in a shard of silence;

The wormy lips of these great, narrow tunnels, the
    pipes,

Are choked with silence;

The banners, the banners, are brittle with decay

And rusted out of colour.

The candles gutter in their sconces,

Curling long welts of evil-smelling smoke about my
     head.

The organ's voice is dead,

Or is it mine?

The banners flap

Like palls upon a bier

On windy midnight burials

Where torches flare a glittering imposture

About the loneliness of violated sod

Gashed open for a grave.

Pity me, then,

Who cry with wingless psalms,

Spellbound in midnight and chill organ pipes.

Above my eyes the banners bleed

Their dripping dust-specks,

Proclaiming the gaunt glories of successful battles.

It would enchant me to see you afloat behind them,

Blown for a moment to an eye-catch.

But who are you to come for frozen hallelujahs!

And yet I go on silently playing.

THE SLIPPERS OF THE GODDESS
OF BEAUTY

"It is easy, like Momus, to find fault with the clattering of the slipper worn by the Goddess of beauty; but 'the serious Gods' found better employment in admiration of her unapproachable loveliness."

THEY clatter, clatter, clatter on the floor,

Her slippers clack upon the marble slabs,

And every time her heels clap, I count one,

And go on counting till my nerves are sick

With one and one and one told out in claps.

He shot a hand out, clutching at my arm

With bony fingers. "Young man," said he, "look up.

Is that a starry face, or am I blind?

Do stars beset her like a crown of pearls?

Does sunset tinge and tangle in her hair,

And moonlight rush in silver from her breasts?

Look well, young man, for maybe I am blind."

I looked, and agony assailed my brain.

He chirruped at me. "So — so! Ancient eyes

Know better than to keep upon the floor.

What dazzles you is kindly sight to me,

One gets accustomed. But I interrupt

Your count. What figure had you reached?" I shook

Him off and staggered to my room, bright pain

Stabbing my head.

             I've never found that count,

Nor started on another. Every day

I look a little longer when she comes,

And see a little more, and bear to see.

But that queer man I've never met again,

Nor very much desired to, perhaps.

Gratitude is an irksome thing to youth,

And I, thank Hermes, am still reckoned young,

Though old enough to look above the floor,

Which is a certain age, I must admit.

But I'll endure that, seeing what it brings.

THE WATERSHED

You say you are my friends,

Coming mistily to greet me in your streets and places,

Handing me roses which are not tinsel surely,

That much is no gainsaying, but there it ends.

For you, the friendly people, are a vision of massed
       faces,

A large wavering smile of something I shrink to call
       derision.

And yet I take your roses demurely

And express my obligation with a nice precision.

Why should I quarrel with what Fate sends?

Poppycock! For indeed I am not a fool.

Next year, perhaps, I shall be no more to you than a
       sick mountebank.

Therefore, while I thank you for your roses,

I hold apart and I too smile,

Bitterly, if you will have it so; but while

I wonder you should laud me for a minute,

I wonder more by what strange finger-rule

You find your praise so easy to be spilt —

The brimful ease of it your chief of poses.

Am I the creature you have swiftly built

Since yesterday, who, formerly, for all you thought,

Printed too light a circle even to round a naught?

Or am I what you'll have me by to-morrow?

There's worry to keep me busy dabbling in it,

And pricks enough to start a pretty sorrow.

Don't think, you polype blur of friendliness,

That any attitude you choose to take

Affects me otherwise than so much less

Than atom's atom. Scarcely for your sake

Would I consent even to notice where

You seem most thickly to invest the air,

Making a coloured rose-bud of the sun.

Your sneers, I think, would leave me well aware

Of something I might boast a bit of having;

Your smooth and pitiless content with what I do

Shows up each whorl and roughness in the grain

Of that harsh article I call my brain,

Of that queer heart all twisted like a shaving

I seldom fret about. So after being

Encumbered for a brief space by your roses

I think to find your subsequent composure

As apt and cheerful as a new disclosure

Broke suddenly across a weary seeing.

Your waning praise will mark a time of day,

And afternoon approaching finds my way

So far advanced, that's all. You are a stage

We reach at ten o'clock and twelve is age.

If I'm an episode, why so are you.

We'll make a kindliness of that — what else is there
      to do?

LA RONDE DU DIABLE

"Here we go round the ivy-bush,"
And that's a tune we all dance to.
Little poet people snatching ivy,
Trying to prevent one another from snatching ivy.
If you get a leaf, there's another for me;
Look at the bush.
But I want your leaf, Brother, and you mine,
Therefore, of course, we push.

"Here we go round the laurel-tree."
Do we want laurels for ourselves most,
Or most that no one else shall have any?
We cannot stop to discuss the question.
We cannot stop to plait them into crowns
Or notice whether they become us.

We scarcely see the laurel-tree,

The crowd about us is all we see,

And there's no room in it for you and me.

Therefore, Sisters, it's my belief

We've none of us very much chance at a leaf.

"Here we go round the barberry-bush."

It's a bitter, blood-red fruit at best,

Which puckers the mouth and burns the heart.

To tell the truth, only one or two

Want the berries enough to strive

For more than he has, more than she.

An acid berry for you and me.

Abundance of berries for all who will eat,

But an aching meat.

That's poetry.

And who wants to swallow a mouthful of sorrow?

The world is old and our century

Must be well along, and we've no time to waste.

Make haste, Brothers and Sisters, push

With might and main round the ivy-bush,

Struggle and pull at the laurel-tree,

And leave the barberries be

For poor lost lunatics like me,

Who set them so high

They overtop the sun in the sky.

Does it matter at all that we don't know why?

MORNING SONG, WITH DRUMS

THE pheasants cry in the dawn,
Mocking the glitter of the nearby city
Struck upon the sky.

Ivy in a wind,
Smooth grass,
Old cedar-trees.

Change is a bitter thing to contemplate
Across a grey dawn.
Puff-ball world, forsooth,
A kick and it is broken into smoke.

The pheasant's cry is raucous in the dawn.

A GRAVE SONG

I'VE a pocketful of emptiness for you, my Dear.

I've a heart like a loaf was baked yesteryear,

I've a mind like ashes spilt a week ago,

I've a hand like a rusty, cracked corkscrew.

Can you flourish on nothing and find it good?

Can you make petrifaction do for food?

Can you warm yourself at ashes on a stone?

Can you give my hand the cunning which has gone?

If you can, I will go and lay me down

And kiss the edge of your purple gown.

I will rise and walk with the sun on my head.

Will you walk with me, will you follow the dead?

A RHYME OUT OF MOTLEY

"I GRASPED a thread of silver; it cut me to the bone —
    I reached for an apple; it was bleak as a stone —
    I reached for a heart, and touched a raw blade —
    And this was the bargain God had made
    For a little gift of speech
    Set a cubit higher than the common reach,
    A debt running on until the fool is dead."

Carve a Pater Noster to put at his head
As a curse or a prayer,
And leave him there.

THE RED KNIGHT

I SAW him,

Standing in red armour before an altar

Under the fish-scale roof of a church

In a river valley in mid-France.

The organ was crying an anthem along the great nave

And the eddy of it tickled the noses of the impish
stone manikins with foxes' tails curled beneath
the architraves.

When the organ ceased crying, he lifted his head

And gazed through the clear-story windows at the
white-blue of an after-rain sky.

Suddenly a thin scatter of sunlight smote upon his
armour

And it flamed like a bonfire, and he in the midst, un-
noticing.

White wood of poplar beneath green bark,

A man, the height and spread of a tall man,

Beneath a burning armour.

I would have flung my kerchief to him to bind upon
his helmet,

But kerchiefs fall obliquely through backward centuries,

And already the light was growing too dim to see a
silken nothing upon a shadowed floor.

Steel footsteps on stone make a strange sound;

I never heard the like before, and I think I never shall
again.

For which unreasonable reason

I am determined to remain a virgin.

NUIT BLANCHE

I want no horns to rouse me up to-night,
And trumpets make too clamorous a ring
To fit my mood, it is so weary white
I have no wish for doing any thing.

A music coaxed from humming strings would please;
Not plucked, but drawn in creeping cadences
Across a sunset wall where some Marquise
Picks a pale rose amid strange silences.

Ghostly and vaporous her gown sweeps by
The twilight dusking wall, I hear her feet
Delaying on the gravel, and a sigh,
Briefly permitted, touches the air like sleet.

And it is dark, I hear her feet no more.

A red moon leers beyond the lily-tank.

A drunken moon ogling a sycamore,

Running long fingers down its shining flank.

A lurching moon, as nimble as a clown,

Cuddling the flowers and trees which burn like glass.

Red, kissing lips, I feel you on my gown —

Kiss me, red lips, and then pass — pass.

Music, you are pitiless to-night.

And I so old, so cold, so languorously white.

ORIENTATION

WHEN the young ladies of the boarding-school take
  the air,
They walk in pairs, each holding a blush-red parasol
  against the sun.
From my window they look like an ambulating parterre
Of roses, I cannot tell one from one.

There is a certain young person I dream of by night,
And paint by day on little two-by-three inch squares
Of ivory. Which is she? Which of all the parasols in
  sight
Covers the blithe, mocking face which stares
At me from twenty miniatures, confusing the single-
  ness of my delight?

You know my window well enough — the fourth from
 the corner. Oh, you know.
Slant your parasol a bit this way, if you please,
And take for yourself the very correct bow
I make toward the line of demure young ladies
Perambulating the street in a neat row.
It is true I have never seen beneath your parasol,
Therefore my miniatures resemble one another not at
 all.

You must pick yourself like a button-hole bouquet,
And lift the parasol to my face one day,
And let me see you laughing at the sun —
Or at me. Then I will choose the one
Of my twenty miniatures most like you
And destroy the others, with which I shall have no-
 thing more to do.

PANTOMIME IN ONE ACT

CERTAINLY the furniture was of satin-wood,

Painted with a lovely design of strawberry flowers and
heliotrope,

And the carpet was Aubusson, all pinks and golds.

On it stood frail chairs, their seats covered with green
and yellow silk,

A striped pattern, continued and broken in the folds

Of the window-curtains. The clock on the mantel-
piece

Was a gay conceit of porcelain flowers springing from
fantastic sprigs of ormolu,

And in the book-cases that lined the walls, three book-
cases with glass doors and gilded locks, were
volumes bound in blue.

The smell of clipped box floated in from the garden
outside, and the sound of a rake

On gravel stirred the silence with an impression of
placid order

Peacefully repeated through a season and seasons
perhaps, but the odour of the box was an ache

After the same perfection which existed inevitably in
every parterre and border.

Mirrors of a yellow-silver shining topped the consoles
at either end,

Behind twin alabaster vases, and in tarnished and
golden duplicate, a blend

Of fact and potent possibility, the room stretched
dreamily through

Walls that were solid or not as one beheld them,
depending on the point of view.

Sunlight fell on the satin-wood escritoire between the
windows,

And on a single Malmaison rose

And the green Ming vase which held it,

Also on a letter, I suppose.

White paper with ink upon it may be taken for such,
    I opine.

But the letter, being without superscription, could
    hardly be considered mine.

On the whole, I preferred to leave it untouched and
    preserve the nicety of my honour.

(Positively I thought I heard a giggle from the lips of
    the Botticelli Madonna

On the chimney-breast; but that was solely her affair.)

I was a poltroon maybe, or wise with a wisdom which
    haunted the air,

Coquettish reserve, that was it, but brazen armour
    could have stayed me less.

Ah, Madame, did I obey your desire, or possibly dis-
    obey it ruthlessly? I confess

I never became aware of your attitude, for I tiptoed to
    the door,

And left the room which had caught your trick of
    smiling,

Exactly as it was before: a beautiful *entourage*, *bien entendu*,

But to me nothing more.

IN A POWDER CLOSET

EARLY EIGHTEENTH CENTURY

MY very excellent young person,

Since Fate has destined you to play the rôle of coiffeur,

You will permit that I admire your quite unsurpassed
    skill,

Together with your polished, if a trifle over-pro-
    nounced, manners,

Without by an inch lessening the distance

Which the hazard of birth and the artifice of custom

Have placed between us.

My mirror tells me that you are a personable man;

But, indeed, it is my own image in this same mirror

Which most occupies my attention.

That such a subject as I offer

Engages you to put forth your best efforts

Is only natural;

That I should remain indifferent is equally so.

Be satisfied that the exigencies of your profession

Admit you to privileges from which a more exalted
station would exclude you.

My maid will, I am sure, be most happy to accommo-
date herself to your wishes,

She is a worthy girl and entertains a not unjustifiable
belief in my continued recognition of her ser-
vices.

The spray of heliotrope is well placed.

Do you think a patch just here — at the corner of the
eye?

Ah, yes. It adds perceptibly.

You are, Sir, a consummate artist.

To-morrow at four I shall expect you.

ATTITUDE UNDER AN ELM TREE

SEEING that you pass your life playing upon the vir-
 ginals

In an upper chamber with only a slit of a window in it,

I wonder why I,

Roaming the hills on a charger red as maple-leaves,

Should find the thought of you attractive.

You were veiled at the jousting, you remember,

Which enables me to imagine you without let or hin-
 drance from the rigidness of fact;

A condition not unproductive of charm if viewed
 philosophically.

Besides, your window gives upon a walled garden,

Which I can by no means enter without dismounting
 from my maple-red charger,

And this I will not do,

Particularly as the garden belongs indubitably to your
    ancestors.

But I thank you for the spray of myrtle I have wound
    about my sleeve.

As it over-topped the wall,

My plucking it was without malice.

ON READING A LINE UNDERSCORED BY KEATS

IN A COPY OF "PALMERIN OF ENGLAND"

You marked it with light pencil upon a printed page,

And, as though your finger pointed along a sunny path

for my eyes' better direction,

I see "a knight mounted on a mulberry courser and

attired in green armour."

I think the sky is faintly blue, but with a Spring shin-

ing about it,

And the new grass scarcely fetlock high in the meads.

He rides, I believe, alongside an overflown river,

By a path soft and easy to his charger's feet.

My vision confuses you with the green-armoured

knight:

So dight and caparisoned might you be in a land of

Faery.

Thus, with denoting finger, you make of yourself an
      escutcheon to guide me to that in you which is
      its essence.
But for the rest,
The part which most persists and is remembered,
I only know I compass it in loving and neither have,
      nor need, a symbol.

THE HUMMING-BIRDS

Up — up — water shooting,

Jet of water, white and silver,

Tinkling with the morning sun-bells.

Red as sun-blood, whizz of fire,

Shock of fire-spray and water.

It is the humming-birds flying against the stream of
the fountain.

The trumpet-vine bursts into a scatter of humming-
birds,

The scarlet-throated trumpet flowers explode with
humming-birds.

The fountain waits to toss them diamonds.

I clasp my hands over my heart

Which will not let loose its humming-birds,

Which will not break to green and ruby,

Which will not let its wings touch air.

Pound and hammer me with irons,

Crack me so that flame can enter,

Pull me open, loose the thunder

Of wings within me.

Leave me wrecked and consoled,

A maker of humming-birds

Who dare bathe in a leaping water.

SUMMER NIGHT PIECE

THE garden is steeped in moonlight,

Full to its high edges with brimming silver,

And the fish-ponds brim and darken

And run in little serpent lights soon extinguished.

Lily-pads lie upon the surface, beautiful as the tarnish-
        ings on frail old silver,

And the Harvest moon droops heavily out of the sky,

A ripe, white melon, intensely, magnificently, shining.

Your window is orange in the moonlight,

It glows like a lamp behind the branches of the old
        wistaria,

It burns like a lamp before a shrine,

The small, intimate, familiar shrine

Placed reverently among the bricks

Of a much-loved garden wall.

WIND AND SILVER

GREATLY shining,

The Autumn moon floats in the thin sky;

And the fish-ponds shake their backs and flash their

dragon scales

As she passes over them.

NIGHT CLOUDS

THE white mares of the moon rush along the sky

Beating their golden hoofs upon the glass Heavens;

The white mares of the moon are all standing on their
       hind legs

Pawing at the green porcelain doors of the remote
       Heavens.

Fly, Mares!

Strain your utmost,

Scatter the milky dust of stars,

Or the tiger sun will leap upon you and destroy you

With one lick of his vermilion tongue.

FUGITIVE

SUNLIGHT,

Three marigolds,

And a dusky purple poppy-pod —

Out of these I made a beautiful world.

Will you have them —

Brightness,

Gold,

And a sleep with dreams?

They are brittle pleasures certainly,

But where can you find better?

Roses are not noted for endurance,

And only thirty days are June.

THE SAND ALTAR

WITH a red grain and a blue grain, placed in precisely
the proper positions, I made a beautiful god, with
plumes of yard-long feathers and a swivel eye.

And with a red grain and a blue grain, placed in precisely the proper positions, I made a dragon, with
scaly wings and a curling, iniquitous tail.

Then I reflected:
If, with the same materials, I can make both
god and dragon, of what use is the higher mathe-
matics?

Having said this, I went outdoors and stood under a
tree and listened to the frogs singing their evening
songs in the green darkness.

TIME–WEB

THE day is sharp and hurried
As wind upon a dahlia stem;
It is harsh and abrupt with me
As a North-east breeze
Striking a bed of sunflowers.
Why should I break at the root
And cast all my fragile flowers in the dust —
I who am no taller than a creeping pansy?
I should be sturdy and definite,
Yet am I tossed, and agitated, and pragmatically
    bending.

PREFACE TO AN OCCASION

How witless to assail the carven halls
Of memory! To climb the high stone steps,
Picking a foothold through the crisp, dry leaves
Whirled in the corners, crunching under foot
Those scattered in the centre, to clap at doors
With battered hauberk, till some seneschal,
Drowsy with age and oversleeping, creaks
Them open an inhospitable inch,
And, grumbling, lets himself be pushed aside
By a determined entrance! Where's the sense
Of striding by tarnished furniture from one
Mournful deserted chamber to another,
Seeking for roses in a vase of dust,
For tapestries where rusty armour hangs,
For blithe allurement under spider-spun

Ceilings corroded to a dripping ash?

What can you find here? A little powdered dust

To pinch up with your finger and your thumb

And fasten in a knotted handkerchief!

Look from the window, Friend, the sky is blue,

The leafless trees blow to a merry wind,

Your horse is tethered at the stairway's foot,

He twitches at the skipping of the leaves.

Pocket your handkerchief and ride away.

Was the trip worth while? I'll wager guinea gold

Within a week you'll wish you had not come,

And send your handkerchief knotted to the wash.

Life's the great cynic, and there's an end of that.

PRIMAVERA

SPRING has arrived.

It is no use your telling me to look at the calendar,

And saying that it is five good days to the twenty-
first of March.

Is the year bound to obey the almanac-makers?

O model of all egregious pedants!

Would you shackle Spring to times and seasons,

And catch her back by her long green skirt

Till the moment you have planned for her?

She has stolen a march this year, for certain.

To-day, at sunrise, I saw a white-breasted nut-hatch

Running up the branch of the oak-tree

That was so broken by the ice-storm last December,

And in the garden a pheasant was picking grains

Out of the manure covering the garden-beds.

There is a snowdrop up by the porch,

Shot clean through the tulip-straw;

And the crows are all agog over my neighbour's pine-
trees.

It is a game of catch-who-catch-can with that green
skirt then.

Even though, in your passion for order, you bring
about a snow storm to-morrow,

It will not matter to me.

This morning, beyond the shadow of a doubt, I saw
the Spring.

KATYDIDS

SHORE OF LAKE MICHIGAN

KATYDIDS scraped in the dim trees,

And I thought they were little white skeletons

Playing the fiddle with a pair of finger-bones.

How long is it since Indians walked here,

Stealing along the sands with smooth feet?

How long is it since Indians died here

And the creeping sands scraped them bone from bone?

Dead Indians under the sands, playing their bones
against strings of wampum.

The roots of new, young trees have torn their graves
asunder,

But in the branches sit little white skeletons

Rasping a bitter death-dirge through the August
night.

TO CARL SANDBURG

I THINK I am cousin-german to Endymion,
Certainly I have loved the moon a long time.

I have seen her, a faint conceit of silver,
Shooting little silver arrows into a marsh pool at
    twilight.
I have seen her, high, round, majestic,
Making herself a jewel of fire out of a sea bay.
I have seen the morning moon, grievously battered,
Limping down a coloured sky.
To-night I saw an evening moon
Dodging between tree-branches
Through a singing silence of crickets,
And a man was singing songs to a black-backed
    guitar.

To-day I saw a country I knew well but had never
    seen.
A country where corn runs a mile or more to a tree-
    line,
A country where a river, brown as bronze, streaked
    green with the flowing heads of water-plants,
Slips between a field of apples and a field of wheat.
A country where the eye seeks a long way
And comes back on the curve of a round sky,
Satisfied with greens and blues, tired with the stretch
    and exhilarated by it.

The moon stops a moment in a hole between leaves
And tells me a new story,
The story of a man who lives in a house with a pear-
    tree before the door,
A story of little green pears changing and ripen-
    ing,

Of long catalpa pods turning yellow through September days.

There is a woman in the house, and children,

And, out beyond, the corn-fields are sleeping and the trees are whispering to the fire-flies.

So I have seen the man's country, and heard his songs before there are words to them.

And the moon said to me: "This now I give you," and went on, stepping through the leaves.

And the man went on singing, picking out his accompaniment softly on the black-backed guitar.

IF I WERE FRANCESCO GUARDI

I

I THINK you are a white clematis
Climbing the wall of a seaside garden,
When there is a green haze on the water
And a boy is eating a melon in a boat with a brown
　　　sail.

II

I think you are the silver heart of a great square,
Holding little people like glass beads,
Watching them parade — parade — and gather,
When the sun slips to an opposite angle,
And a thunder of church bells lies like a bronze roof
　　　beneath the sky.

ELEONORA DUSE

I

SEEING's believing, so the ancient word
Chills buds to shrivelled powder flecks, turns flax
To smoky heaps of straw whose small flames wax
Only to gasp and die. The thing's absurd!
Have blind men ever seen or deaf men heard?
What one beholds but measures what one lacks.
Where is the prism to draw gold from blacks,
Or flash the iris colours of a bird?
Not in the eye, be sure, nor in the ear,
Nor in an instrument of twisted glass,
Yet there are sights I see and sounds I hear
Which ripple me like water as they pass.
This that I give you for a dear love's sake
Is curling noise of waves marching along a lake.

II

A letter or a poem — the words are set

To either tune. Be careful how you slice

The flap which is held down by this device

Impressed upon it. In one moment met

A cameo, intaglio, a fret

Of workmanship, and I. Like melted ice

I took the form and froze so, turned precise

And brittle seal, a creed in silhouette.

Seeing's believing? What then would you see?

A chamfered dragon? Three spear-heads of steel?

A motto done in flowered charactry?

The thin outline of Mercury's winged heel?

Look closer, do you see a name, a face,

Or just a cloud dropped down before a holy place?

III

Lady, to whose enchantment I took shape

So long ago, though carven to your grace,

Bearing, like quickened wood, your sweet sad face

Cut in my flesh, yet may I not escape

My limitations: words that jibe and gape

After your loveliness and make grimace

And travesty where they should interlace

The weave of sun-spun ocean round a cape.

Pictures then must contain you, this and more,

The sigh of wind floating on ripe June hay,

The desolate pulse of snow beyond a door,

The grief of mornings seen as yesterday.

All that you are mingles as one sole cry

To point a world aright which is so much awry.

IV

If Beauty set her image on a stage

And bid it mirror moments so intense

With passion and swift largess of the sense

To a divine exactness, stamp a page

With mottoes of hot blood, and disengage

No atom of mankind's experience,

But lay the soul's complete incontinence

Bare while it tills grief's gusty acreage.

Doing this, you, spon-image to her needs,

She picked to pierce, reveal, and soothe again,

Shattering by means of you the tinsel creeds

Offered as meat to the pinched hearts of men.

So, sacrificing you, she fed those others

Who bless you in their prayers even before their
    mothers.

V

Life seized you with her iron hands and shook

The fire of your boundless burning out

To fall on us, poor little ragged rout

Of common men, till like a flaming book

We, letters of a message, flashed and took

The fiery flare of prophecy, devout

Torches to bear your oil, a dazzling shout,

The liquid golden running of a brook.

Who, being upborne on racing streams of light,

Seeing new heavens sprung from dusty hells,

Considered you, and what might be your plight,

Robbed, plundered — since Life's cruel plan compels

The perfect sacrifice of one great soul

To make a myriad others even a whit more whole.

VI

Seeing you stand once more before my eyes

In your pale dignity and tenderness,

Wearing your frailty like a misty dress

Draped over the great glamour which denies

To years their domination, all disguise

Time can achieve is but to add a stress,

A finer fineness, as though some caress

Touched you a moment to a strange surprise.

Seeing you after these long lengths of years,

I only know the glory come again,

A majesty bewildered by my tears,

A golden sun spangling slant shafts of rain,

Moonlight delaying by a sick man's bed,

A rush of daffodils where wastes of dried leaves spread.